What KIDS Need Most in a MOM

PATRICIA H. RUSHFORD

SPIRE

© 1986, 1999 by Patricia H. Rushford

Published by Fleming H. Revell
a division of Baker Book House Company
P.O. Box 6287, Grand Rapids, MI 49516-6287

Spire edition published 2002

Printed in the United States of America

ISBN 0-8007-8684-X

Scripture quotations identified KJV are from the King James Version of the Bible.

Scripture quotations identified RSV are from the Revised Standard Version of the
Bible, copyright 1946, 1952, 1971 by the Division of Christian Education of the
National Council of the Churches of Christ in the USA. Used by permission.

Scripture quotations identified TEV are from Today's English Version. Copyright
© American Bible Society 1966, 1971, 1976, 1992. Used by permission.

Scripture quotations identified TLB are from *The Living Bible* © 1971. Used by permission of Tyndale House Publishers, Inc., Wheaton, IL 60189. All rights reserved.

Material from *Have You Hugged Your Teenager Today?* by Patricia H. Rushford,
copyright © 1983 by Patricia H. Rushford. Published by Fleming H. Revell, a division of Baker Book House.

For current information about all releases from Baker Book House, visit our web
site:

http://www.bakerbooks.com

What KIDS
Need Most in a
MOM

By Patricia H. Rushford

NONFICTION

What Kids Need Most in a Mom
Have You Hugged Your Teenager Today?
Jack & Jill Syndrome: Healing for Broken Children
Caring for Your Elderly Parents
Emotional Phases of a Woman's Life

FICTION

Morningsong (A romantic suspense)

Jennie McGrady Mystery Series

Too Many Secrets	*Betrayed*
The Silent Witness	*In Too Deep*
Pursued	*Over the Edge*
Deceived	*From the Ashes*
Without a Trace	*Desperate Measures*
Dying to Win	

The Helen Bradley Mysteries
Now I Lay Me Down to Sleep
Red Sky in Mourning
A Haunting Refrain

To David and Caryl and all of my wonderful grandchildren

Contents

Part 1

Mything Out on Motherhood

Part 2

The Treasures of a Mother's Heart

Part 3

What's a Mother to Do?

Acknowledgments

A special thanks to all the moms and kids who shared their stories and ideas with me.

Introduction

Not long ago, my publisher called and asked if I would be interested in revising and updating *What Kids Need Most in a Mom.* The book has been quite successful since its release in 1986, and they wanted to bring it out again. I was thrilled. I've written about thirty books now—both fiction and nonfiction. I must say that of all the nonfiction books I've written, *What Kids Need Most in a Mom* is my favorite. I think that's because I get so many calls and letters from moms who tell me how much the book has helped them through difficult periods in their lives. One such mother called me one evening at the end of her rope: "I'm so sorry to bother you, but I'm desperate and don't see how I can go on anymore. I didn't know who else to call. You see, I've been reading your book, and I just knew you'd understand."

She went on to tell me about her problems in trying to rear four children and go to school and work. I listened with an empathetic ear and was able to give her reassurance and support. When she hung up she thanked me. Her problems remained much as they had been when she called, but she could now go back to them with renewed strength.

Another woman, whom I met while speaking to a MOPS (Mothers of Preschoolers) gathering, told me she'd read my book during one of the lowest moments of her life. "I was sick and tired of parenting books that made me feel guilty," she said. "A friend gave me your book and told me to give it

11

a try. I told her I would but also warned her that if it didn't help I was throwing it in the ocean." She smiled. "It was great. You didn't make me feel guilty. I recommend it to other moms all the time."

I've been a mother for thirty-four years now. My children are all grown up with children of their own. At this writing I have nine grandchildren. I've experienced the joys and the heartaches of seeing my children grow and develop into mature adults—wondering at times if they ever would. I was not a perfect mother, and there are many things I'd do differently if given a chance to do it all again. Not long ago I began to confess my shortcomings as a mother to my daughter, Caryl.

She smiled and said, "You couldn't have been all that bad; look at how great I turned out."

And she has. She's a wonderful mom with four great kids. I taught her well. And if she wants to see me as a great mom— far be it from me to disillusion her.

What Kids Need Most in a Mom is a book that not only offers practical help and advice, it also offers encouragement and hope. In the end you will not be perfect. Despite what the Mother's Day cards claim, real mothers seldom are. But, hopefully, you will come out stronger and more self-assured, and determined to be the best mom you can be.

In the words of Harriet Beecher Stowe, "I long to put the experience of fifty years at once into your young lives, to give you at once the key of that treasure chamber every gem of which has cost me tears and struggles and prayers, but you must work for these inward treasures yourselves."

My prayer is that *What Kids Need Most in a Mom* will help you to that end.

1

Musings of Another Mother

Becoming a mom comes easily enough for most of us. You get pregnant and poof, you're a mother. Being the mom your kids need, however, is not quite so easy. While giving birth to a baby is considered labor, the true labor starts when you bring your baby home and begin the sometimes painful process of mothering.

Writing a book about kids and what they need most in a mom was not an easy task, especially for an imperfect mom. But there were thoughts and ideas I wanted to share, pitfalls I wanted mothers to avoid, stories I wanted to tell . . . so I set to the task, eager to get it all into my computer.

I'd no sooner started writing when the phone rang. It was my son, David, calling from California—I live in Washington.

"Hi, Mom," he said with a smile in his voice. "What's up?" (He starts all his calls that way.)

"Nothing much," I gave my usual answer.

"I got a new job."

"Really? That's good." I was wishing he were closer to home and maybe going to college. But I didn't say so.

"How's Dad?"

"Fine. He's playing basketball. He'll be sorry he missed you."

"Well, tell him I said hi . . . and that I love him."

"I will." I paused for a moment. "Dave? I have some good news. I'm writing another book."

"Oh yeah?"

"It's called *What Kids Need Most in a Mom*. Would you write a paragraph or two for me? You know, tell me what you needed most in a mom."

I suddenly felt embarrassed, shy, and fearful. What if I hadn't fulfilled his needs? What if he looked at me as a failure? I certainly had my down times—times when I yelled too much or didn't pay enough attention.

"Sure, Mom." His warm voice interrupted my phantom fears. "That's easy. You're the best mom a guy could have."

We talked a bit longer and hung up. I was elated. Do you have any idea what it means to hear your grown son say you were the best? Of course you do. My goodness. His comment would lift my spirits for months. And it wasn't even Mother's Day.

Even though my son's words warmed me, I knew they weren't entirely true. I hadn't been the best. It wasn't from lack of trying. But it's the final analysis that counts. If my son wants to think I'm the best, I'm certainly not going to argue the point.

If I'd Known Then What I Know Now

Almost any mom who's been around for a while will agree that being a mom is a learning process. By the time we get this business of mothering pretty well figured out, our kids have become adults who don't think they need to be mothered anymore and who, strangely enough, begin to parent us. Now that I think I know what kids need most in a mom, mine are all grown up and have children of their own.

Even so, they often call asking for advice or encouragement, or just to talk. They talk about dreams and plans, about careers and marriage and having babies. While they don't need me to nurture them in the way I did when they were younger, they still need a mom.

Pigtails and Super Glue

I met my good friend Linda, mother of three children under six, for lunch one day. I was still euphoric over the phone call from my son.

"How neat," Linda said. "Your kids always share with you and let you know what's happening, don't they?"

I nodded. "About once a week." Then, remembering a time they weren't always so thoughtful, I said, "They're improving with age."

"I hope my kids will care about me and want my advice when they grow up. But then, you've got an edge on parenting, I mean being a nurse and all. That must have helped."

"I suppose, that and the fact that I could have opened a library with all the pop psychology books I bought on child rearing."

"How did you do when they were two?"

"I'd rather not talk about it. Why do you ask?"

"Oh, I don't know." Linda frowned. "Sometimes I feel like I'm doing great as a mom. Other times I feel as if they'd be better off being raised in the jungle by a mama hyena."

"Well, they'd get a lot of laughs that way."

"Very funny."

"Mothering hasn't been easy for me, either," I said. "I went through some hard times figuring out the ingredients that go into the making of a mom." I leaned forward and rested my elbows on the table.

"Well, in that case, tell me what you know so I won't have to learn everything the hard way."

"You want my life story over lunch?"

"I'm serious. What do you know now that you didn't know then and wish you had? Did that make sense?"

I laughed. "Yeah. You want me to tell you what I would do differently if I could do it all again. You want me to tell you about my mistakes so you won't make them. And you want me to tell you about the things that worked so you can try them."

"Right."

"Since that would take a bit longer than our lunch break, why don't I write you a book—I was thinking about doing one anyway."

"Great idea, but don't write it just for me. I know a lot of moms who need all the help they can get. You could call it *Real Moms Don't Eat Baby Food*."

"Cute." I chuckled. "I'll lay it on my publisher. Did you? Eat baby food, I mean?"

"I'm not telling."

"Oh, come on . . . I'll confess if you do."

"What, and blow my image? Not a chance."

Knowing I wasn't going to get the confession I wanted and understanding her need to save face, I changed the subject. "I think we're going to title it *What Kids Need Most in a Mom*."

"Not bad. Let me know when it comes out. I know a couple dozen moms right now, including me, who could use it. But hurry, will you? This has been one heck of a day. Jeremy needed something different for show-and-tell, so he took my sewing shears and cut off Penny's pigtails."

"You're kidding. What did you do?"

"I swatted his bottom and yelled a lot. Then I cried.

"He patted my arm and said, 'I'm sorry, Mommy, I won't do it again.' I hugged him and said I hoped not. I went to wash my face, and when I came back into the kitchen, Jeremy and Penny were grinning like Cheshire cats. 'Jay fix it, Mommy,' Penny said. She turned around to show me. Two lopsided tails hung from her tousled curls, held in place with gobs of Super Glue."

Practical Help for Moms

Linda was right. There are a lot of mothers who need the practical help and encouragement my book offers. (I certainly could have used a book like this when I was younger.) Oh, and guilt—guilt is like an addiction to so many moms. They need to get it out of their systems. I'll wean them off guilt and start them on solids like forgiveness and contentment.

I'll offer time-tested advice and actual case studies from my thirty-five years of firsthand experience. To that, of course, I'll add the advice my kids gave me. (They were never too shy to tell me when they thought I'd done something wrong.)

Let's move into part 1 of this book and take a close look at the myths that make a lot of moms feel as if they're in danger of failing motherhood.

Mything Out on Motherhood

Are you *mything* out on motherhood because you can't live up to all the expectations piled on top of you? Do you find yourself spinning hopelessly on a merry-go-round of responsibilities that seems to be going nowhere fast? Have you had it up to your hair follicles with ideal-parenting theories? Are you located somewhere under a ton of guilt, but can't quite figure out where?

Before we try the keys that can lead to better mothering, let's take a look at those timeworn myths and ideals that so often put us moms in seemingly impossible places.

In chapter 2 we'll talk about the mythical, mystical, magical mom. She's the lady in the Mother's Day cards who can do no wrong and whose perfection has, at times, made many moms, including me, feel like a lily at the bottom of a dung heap.

Chapter 3 will explore the facade of the perfect parent and hopefully keep you from falling off the pedestal of high ideals.

The fourth chapter will expose the ever-popular and intimidating "Super Mom" for who she really is—a threat to our children and to our sanity.

2

The Mythical, Mystical, Magical Mom

There is one holiday that strikes fear in the hearts of mothers everywhere. Mother's Day. It's that day when we must stand up and be measured against the standards set forth on millions of cards.

On Mother's Day I usually wake up with a headache. Will anyone remember that I'm a mother? Did my behavior over the past year warrant a gift from the kids?

A few years ago, I experienced a Mother's Day that started out to be one of the worst days of my life. It didn't feel like Mother's Day. It seemed more like winter. The nest was empty, my branches barren. Months—years ago—my seedlings flew into the wind. My son, then nineteen, had struck out on his own.

I woke up that morning thinking of him, wondering if he'd call to wish me a happy Mother's Day. If guilt had been a racket, I'd have been the ball being beaten against the wall.

Throughout the morning, my memory drifted back to every mistake I'd ever made as a mother. Nothing seemed bad enough to deserve this—being neglected on Mother's Day.

I decided to give him the benefit of the doubt. Perhaps he'd forgotten. Then I realized that with all the hype from advertisers, he'd have to be isolated in the remote regions of Tibet not to remember.

"He must have been in an accident," I mused. "Why else would he forget me?" Then I decided he'd *better* have been in an accident because that was the only excuse I could accept.

The day was drawing to a close. It was two in the afternoon and not a word from him. By this time I was getting angry. Then guilt whopped me again. I felt bad by the time four o'clock rolled around.

At 4:10 the doorbell rang. The florist delivered a long-stemmed red rose. For me? I closed the door, hardly daring to breathe. Could it be? I read the card. "Happy Mother's Day" was written in fancy script letters across the top. Beneath the formal heading the bold scrawl said, "I love you, Mom."

What did I do? You guessed it. I sat down and bawled. A short time later David called.

"Did you get the rose?"

"Oh, yes. Thank you so much."

"Is it nice?"

"It's beautiful. They put it in a milk glass vase and tucked in baby's breath and a feathery fern."

"That's neat." After a few minutes of catching me up on his latest escapades, he announced, "Well, I gotta go. I just wanted to call and see if it came and tell you I love you."

What can I say? He remembered. What I'd nearly pegged as one of the worst days of my life turned out to be one of the best.

I couldn't help thinking about this idea of Mother's Day and the expectations that go with it. So often our impression of real motherhood is mixed up in our *mythtaken* identity of what we think a mom ought to be.

Especially for Moms

Every year on the second Sunday in May, we celebrate Mother's Day. It is a day set aside to honor mothers everywhere. Never mind the fact that your family tells you: "Leave the dishes today, Mom. It's Mother's Day and you shouldn't be working. You can do them tomorrow."

Try not to mourn the fact that secretaries and pickles receive one full week of national acclaim, while we, like groundhogs, get only one day.

Instead, hold dear to your heart:

- The piece of plaster imprinted with your Cynthia's tiny hand
- Kevin's stick-figure portrait of you in your new purple hat, big red eyes with five long, straight lashes, and green teeth
- Angel's heart-shaped bookmark that says, "I love you, Mom," written in macaroni letters

It is these gifts, created in love by your child's inexperienced hands, that make being a mother worthwhile.

Yet that is not what merchandisers across the country want us to believe. Take a look at the racks of Mother's Day cards and paraphernalia overflowing the stores in March and April and into May. The merchants make a bundle, reaping the harvest off the guilt seeds they planted in us.

The Guilt Trip of the Century

Mother's Day was originally designed to honor Mom with love. Commercialism has made Mother's Day the greatest contributing factor to guilt in this century. Kids of all ages feel guilt when Mother's Day rolls around—me included. I'd love to be able to hand over to Mother the keys to a new Porsche or even a microwave oven. But who can afford it?

As a mother, on the other hand, I wonder if my kids will remember me. What lovely gift will I be blessed with this year? The only one who could afford that Norwegian silver fox jacket is my husband, but if he's told me once he's told me a hundred times, "You're not my mother."

I feel guilty and a bit selfish about where my thoughts have taken me. After all, I should be thrilled with any kind of remembrance, even if it's just a hug. Aren't those kinds of gifts the best? At least that's what I always told my kids. Maybe I shouldn't have been so hasty.

I try not to watch as someone else's son buys his mother a giant-screen television set, complete with a satellite dish. "After all," I muse, "he's probably just appeasing his guilt over not speaking to her all year."

Then there are the cards. How can mothers read the flowery descriptions of what we're supposed to be and not feel guilty?

According to the cards, mothers are *sunshine, laughter, moonlight,* and *roses.* Mothers are *ever faithful, enduring, strong,* and *compassionate.*

Quite frankly, verses on Mother's Day cards make me want to do two things: first, salute and recite the scouts' motto ("On my honor I will do my best to do my duty"); second, throw up.

We've Created a Monster

Over the years we have come to believe in this superior, mythical being. Mothers often believe if they try hard enough they can achieve the ultimate level of motherhood. When we fail we feel guilty and may even end up in the dark dungeons of low self-esteem.

Believing in the ideal mom is not without its hazards for the kids too. "Strangely enough, it is the overidealization of the maternal instinct which accounts for the thousands of neglected children among us," writes Ruth Herschberger in

Adam's Rib.[1] While this isn't the only reason for abused and neglected children, she certainly has a point.

The ideal-mother image brings guilt. Guilt often causes us to turn away from the problem—the children. When we can't live up to our expectations (and society's) we often resort to blaming others for our inadequacies. We may begin to think, *If only the kids would shape up, I could be like "her."*

Children often feel cheated because their mother doesn't meet the qualifications set forth on the cards.

Thus we find ourselves competing with "Everybody Else's Mom." By hanging on to the ideal, we've created a monster.

Erma Bombeck, in her book *Motherhood: The Second Oldest Profession,* describes her this way:

> She has no name. Her phone number is unlisted. But she exists in the mind of every child who has ever tried to get his own way and used her as a last resort. Everybody Else's Mother is right out of the pages of Greek mythology—mysterious, obscure, and surrounded by hearsay. . . . She is the answer to every child's prayer. . . . She likes snakes, ice cream before dinner, and unmade beds. . . . She lives in the hearts of children everywhere who have to believe that somewhere there is an adult on their side.[2]

Motherhood, the American Flag, and Apple Pie

Mom is the American Dream, right up there with the flag and apple pie. We are told that from her womb comes the dream of future peace and a perfect nation of brave, creative, intelligent, happy, generous, and "good" people.

Yet, corny as it may sound, there is a part of each one of us that secretly believes in what Pope Pius XII referred to as the "crown of creation . . . expression of all that is best, kindest, most lovable here below." I long to give that perfect kind of mother love.

As a young mother perfect love poured around me like a rainbow, but I couldn't grasp it. It hovered, perpetually out of reach. I would judge myself by that standard and feel like a failure.

Then I realized it was like believing that somehow I could be as perfect, right, and just as God Himself. If that were the case, though, why would we need God?

While I believe in striving to be the best mother I can be, I have learned not to feel intimidated or guilt ridden by descriptions of the perfect mother.

So what is all this leading to? Am I out to abolish Mother's Day, or (gasp) motherhood? Heaven forbid. No, nothing so drastic. I only point out these poetic and idealistic impressions of motherhood to say that is precisely what they are— poetic, idealistic impressions. They are a child's illusion—a blend of ingredients that, if measured in the exact proportions, could create the perfect mother.

Although few of us can be ideal moms (believe it or not, I've met a few who thought they were), we take our role of mothering seriously. We try to be better mothers by learning what our kids need most in us.

I used to believe in the mythical, mystical, magical mom. But I eventually learned to dig my way out from under the dung heap of high ideals, accept myself for being an imperfect but okay person, and become more like the mom my kids really needed.

If you're a mom who finds herself held under by piles of high expectations, there's only one solution—start digging.

3

Real Moms Don't Eat Baby Food

When I first stepped into my role as Mother, I really believed in the ideal mom. I knew if I tried hard enough I could be all sweetness and light, kind and gentle, slow to anger and eternally loving. There were certain spoken and unspoken rules I had learned from society about mothering and now it was my turn to apply them. Society led me to believe I could be better than other mothers who had gone before me.

I built a pedestal out of my confidence and the "expert" child-rearing advice I'd read. Then, feeling highly competent, I took my place at the top.

It's a Long Way to the Ground

I wish someone had told me about the dangers of pedestal thinking. If I'd been able to see into the future, I'd have climbed off before it was too late. But I stubbornly clung to my lofty notions of what the perfect mom would be.

"A real mom," I said to myself, "would never relinquish the care of her baby to others. Only a mother can properly meet her baby's needs.

"Real moms don't yell at their kids.

"Real moms don't resort to fits of temper.

"Real moms don't have to spank their kids, because if children are brought up correctly, spankings are unnecessary."

These were only a few of the beliefs that held my pedestal together.

It was only a matter of weeks, however, before I noticed a crack in my plaster base.

I Was a Baby Food Junkie

This isn't easy to admit, but . . . I was a closet baby food eater—a real baby food junkie. I never bought a jar of baby food I wouldn't eat myself. While other mothers might have simply touched it with their tongues to make certain it wasn't too hot, I got hooked. For every bite that went into my kid, half went into me.

Oh, it started innocently enough. I mean, I had to show my kid the food was edible, didn't I? When my firstborn was six months old I began to wean him off the breast onto some solid foods. I made all the usual "mom" noises.

"C'mon, sweetheart, eat your num-num."

"Da!" David grinned and shook his head as he whopped the high-chair tray with his fist.

"It's good, honey. See?" I put the spoon to my mouth for a taste so he could see I wasn't trying to poison him.

"Mmmm." I took another spoonful. Applesauce. "Mmmm! Hey, this stuff isn't bad," I said, taking a bigger spoonful. When he saw that I really did like it, he clamored for his share. I don't think he was particularly happy with the way I divided our portions—one for him and one, two for me, but he couldn't argue. I was his mom and I was bigger.

One day he threw a tantrum over my eating the whole jar of cherry vanilla pudding before offering him a bite. From that day on I knew I had to change my ways. I kept all the cherry vanilla for myself and ate it when he was asleep.

Fortunately, after Caryl, my second and last child, went to table food, I was forced to give up my habit.

The rest is history. One by one, my parenting theories disintegrated and my pedestal (with me on it) toppled to the ground. Let's take a look at some of those shaky ideals right now.

Only a mother . . .

Somewhere along the way I'd picked up the notion that only a mother is qualified to adequately supply the child's needs. Mothers are the nurturers, the primary caregivers. Fathers and grandparents will do in a pinch. Baby-sitters are a last resort. No one can care for a child like a mother.

I believed that mothers somehow had that special something no one else had. A touch—the sound of mom's voice was the only thing that could quiet a crying infant. Only mom can kiss an owie and make it feel better. I suppose in a sense that's true.

You may be wondering what I'm getting at here. Of course mothers are special. Children need their mothers and we are responsible for their care. But they don't need their mothers exclusively. In today's busy world, mothers who believe this myth will end up feeling guilty and overworked. The plan here is not to downplay a mother's worth, but to get fathers and other family members more involved in your child's care.

I'll be honest and tell you that I rather liked being the only one my babies came to for comfort. I took a certain amount of pride in the fact that I was the only person who could rock them to sleep. They depended on me. It does a mother's heart good to feel that sense of power when baby cries as you walk away, or reaches up to you for comfort—when no one else will do.

At the same time I felt frustrated and overwrought at times because I didn't want to carry the entire burden alone.

The *only mom* myth can be detrimental to moms and kids as well as to dads. It creates stress and eats into the valuable time every mother needs to recharge. It keeps men from developing their nurturing instincts and children from bonding with other people. We can't afford to think that we are indispensable and that other people in our children's lives are not really necessary. Believing that I'm the only one who can care for my child is really an unhealthy way of looking at parenting.

I remember when my daughter left her little one, Hannah, then six months old, with my husband and me for a weekend. Hannah cried for hours. It was her first time ever away from Mom and she didn't like it one bit. Though she knew us and had on occasion even allowed us to hold her, she wanted Mom and no one else would do. By the end of the weekend she was fine and had come to accept us, but what a traumatic time it was for her and for us.

I don't believe any of us was ever meant to be the sole caregiver. An old African saying states, "It takes a village to raise a child." While bonding to Mom is essential to a child's growth and development, it is also important that the child have bonds with other family members—especially Dad.

Don't quote me on this, but frankly, I think the culprits who snowed mothers with the "only mothers" philosophy were fathers. Think about it. Maybe way back in the annals of time, perhaps even as far back as Adam, Father took one look at his tiny, wiggly little baby and said, "He's so little. I'm so strong I might hurt the little tyke. Here, you take him." Then a few days later, can't you just picture Junior messing his diaper and Mom saying, "Dear, I'm up to my armpits in dirty dishes. Could you change the baby?"

Daddy takes one look at the mustardy ooze and gags. "Oh . . . ah, honey, I'm not so sure I should do this. My hands are so big and clumsy, I'm afraid I'll stick him with a pin."

Is it possible that men, filled with the fear of failure, and seeing a perfect cop-out, felt justified in handing the role of nurturer over to Mom?

On the other hand, maybe it was Mom who decided that the child's father did not have the skills to take care of baby. Maybe we moms, enjoying the heady sensation of being the only person baby would come to, created the myth on our own. Women love to feel needed. Why wouldn't a mother, even though she complains about the workload, be subconsciously pleased that only she can meet the needs of her baby?

Maybe the problem lies with both sides. The woman takes charge of child rearing because she has learned the art of nurturing and assumes it is her role. The man sees an opportunity to step aside, so he does. It is, after all, human nature to take the easy road.

Will the child be damaged if we allow others to occasionally do what we assume moms have always done? Probably not. In the book *Mothering,* Rudolph Schaffer writes, "There is nothing to indicate any biological need for an exclusive primary bond, nothing to suggest that mothering cannot be shared by several people."[1]

Yes, our kids need their mommies. That's as it should be, but they can benefit by being cared for by others as well. In many societies, men and women share the responsibility of caring for the children. For example, Wilfried Pelletier, in his book *This Is a Book about Schools,* writes, "In an Indian home, if a child's face is dirty or his diaper is wet, he is picked up by anyone. The mother or father or whoever comes into the house. . . . And children are fed whenever they are hungry. They are never allowed to be in want."[2]

Kids need a mom who will help them to develop socially by encouraging others to contribute to their care. Kids need a mom who is not so insecure and desperate for love, that she clings to the belief that only she can meet her child's needs.

Make Room for Daddy[3]

"Isn't she the most beautiful baby in the world?" Joy, pride, and wonder fill Ken as he holds his infant daughter for the first time. His father heart bursts with love. He longs to protect her, care for her, nurture her. He wants to do more than provide a paycheck and help out. He wants to be part of her life but hasn't a clue how to accomplish it.

Most dads want to be involved in caring for baby, and many waver in uncertainty. Like so many men, Ken's nurturing instincts were never encouraged, his fathering never explored. Men like Ken catered to the myth that caring for baby was Mom's job.

Ken and his wife, Meg, stand at a crossroads faced by new moms and dads every day. Will they fall into the old routine with Mom taking over baby's care and Dad fading into the background? Or will they bond as a family and share the role of parenting? Today, more and more fathers are ignoring stereotypes and are stepping in to do what for years has been considered a mother's role—taking care of baby.

Here are some ways you can help the man in your life take over some of the parenting responsibilities. (For those of you who are single parents, consider getting a close friend or parent to assist in your child's care.)

1. Ask him to share in the pregnancy. Intimacy and bonding begin before baby is born. Learn all you can about pregnancy and childbirth together. Have him go with you to all or at least some of the prenatal exams and plan to attend childbirth preparation classes together so he can empathize with you and assist in the delivery of your child.

2. Share intimate moments. Place his hand on your abdomen so he can feel the baby move. Have him listen to the heartbeat. Encourage him to talk to your baby so the sound of Dad's voice becomes as familiar as Mom's. Share openly your excitement, joy, concerns, and fears with him and encourage

him to do the same. Finally, pray together for a healthy, happy child, a smooth delivery, and a loving partnership.

3. Before the baby comes, prepare for parenthood. Take a parenting class together. Read about babies and learn about their development. Ask questions. Hang around other people's children to get some hands-on experience. Education can prevent feelings of insecurity and inadequacy.

4. Traditionally, friends and relatives shower Mom and baby with gifts, making pregnancy and childbirth a "woman's" thing. Why not suggest a baby shower where both sexes are welcome?

5. When the baby arrives, encourage your husband to take some time off work if possible. Paternity leave is as important as maternity leave but not as easily accepted or granted.

6. Teach him to care for your newborn. Contrary to popular belief, with the exception of childbearing and breastfeeding, a dad can do anything for his baby that a mom can do. Dad can feed and burp your baby—and rock him to sleep. He can change her diapers—even the messy ones.

Even women who long for it may resist their husbands' involvement. Moms may unknowingly become overprotective, bossy, and critical in an attempt to hold on to or maintain control as the primary caregiver. Again, talk about it, share your feelings, and work together toward the goals you both want. Your kids need a mom who knows how important dads are.

Realize How Important Dads Are[4]

"Daddy's home!" Two-year-old Scotty scoots off his mother's lap and attaches himself to his daddy's legs. Bob sets down his briefcase, reaches down, and throws his little buddy in the air.

Scotty squeals with delight. "More, Daddy, more!"

Bob complies. Two, maybe three times before settling his son in his arms and greeting his wife, Pam, with a kiss.

Later Bob will read his son a bedtime story, say prayers, and tuck him in.

Bob takes his fathering responsibilities seriously. He works hard at being the best dad he can be. And that hasn't been easy. "When we first learned that Pam was pregnant, I was thrilled and, at the same time, terrified. I never had a relationship with my dad," Bob admitted. "He divorced my mother when I was five years old. I'd always sworn that when I had kids, I'd be a good father, but when I faced fatherhood for the first time, I had no idea what being a good father meant."

Sadly, many men face fatherhood with similar feelings of fear and inadequacy. Perhaps one of the greatest gifts we moms can give our husbands, and in turn our children, is to help our husbands see how important they are to the little ones in their care.

"More than half of today's children will spend at least part of childhood without a father." When I read this accounting in *U.S. News & World Report,* I was not shocked or surprised by the statistics. I could only nod my head in affirmation.

Does it matter? Are fathers all that important? As long as a child has a loving mother, isn't that enough? As a society we're becoming painfully aware that no, it is not enough. Children need their daddies too. The article in *U.S. News* went on to say, "The absence of fathers is linked to most social nightmares—from boys with guns to girls with babies." We've known for years that maternal deprivation can create serious physical and emotional problems in children. Now we're seeing the effects of *paternal deprivation.* The world is full of children who suffer the effects of not being properly fathered. It is also full of adults who still feel those effects long after childhood has passed.

Dads Can Be Nurturers Too

Children need moms *and* dads who care for and nurture them. If you thought nurturing was a feminine trait, think again. To nurture is to care for, parent, sustain, rear, advance, cultivate, protect, develop, and train. We are all meant to have this Christ-like compassion and love and ability to nurture. It is not a feminine trait but a human trait.

Most dads instinctively want to nurture but waver in uncertainty. Some have no idea how. Their nurturing instincts were never encouraged, their fathering instincts never explored.

Although nurturing is instinctual in all of us, it must be enabled, encouraged, and directed. If your husband didn't learn this from his mom—well, guess what. You may need to help him along or teach him the basics. Or, you might enroll him in Parenting 101 at your local community college.

Control Yourself, You're an Adult

Another kind of mythical thinking has come out of the numerous pop psychology books on the market. According to some experts, anger and other negative emotions must be held in check. Good mothers do not damage their children's psyches by losing control.

For example, say seven-year-old Jack rides his skateboard in the house, trips, and smashes into your china cabinet, breaking several items. You must, as an in-control mother, say (calmly), "Dear, I am a little upset now. Please go outside while I clean this up. When I have had a chance to think it over, we will talk about a suitable punishment."

A well-read, child-care-manual-junkie mother would never swat his bottom or grab the kid by the shoulders and shake him until his teeth rattled, while sputtering, "How many times have I told you not to ride that thing in the house? Now look what you've done!" Nor would she sit on the floor in the middle of the disaster and cry, "My china . . . some of it came from England on the Mayflower . . . it can't be replaced," then sob loudly.

This display of tears and anger might upset the child and cause him to feel remorseful. He might even become compassionate and try to console you. Of course, he is much too young to deal with such extreme emotional responses. We wouldn't want him responding in anger and tears to the wrongs in this world when he grows up, would we?

While I can't condone physical abuse such as teeth-rattling shakings, or beating, I realize that at times we parents mess up. Occasional spankings can be used as a way of punishment, and we should learn to control our emotions to some extent. I can't, however, agree with the idea of total control of your emotions when dealing with children. There must be a natural balance or the child will get mixed messages.

George Bernard Shaw says it well in *Maxims for Revolutionists:* "The best brought-up children are those who have seen their parents as they are. Hypocrisy is not the parent's first duty."

In the same work, he writes, "If you strike a child, take care that you strike in anger . . . a blow in cold blood neither can nor should be forgiven."[5]

Harsh words, but an interesting theory. I don't like to think of striking a child at all. But there are times when spankings may be appropriate.

Let's consider for a moment what Shaw is saying. How often have you read manuals in which you are told to wait until your anger passes before punishing the child? Later, the spanking may be administered if needed.

Have you ever tried to spank a child when you weren't angry? I did—once. It was awful. I felt worse than I had at previous times when, in my spurt of emotion, I reacted in anger and smacked the kid's bottom. In either case, I felt like a rotten mom. I'm not sure whether my guilt came more from striking my child in cold blood or failing to do the "right thing" according to the book.

I just had a thought. Remember when Jesus became righteously angry in the temple? Did He calm down before exacting punishment? Did He compose Himself first, then throw the money changers from the temple? He was angry. He acted in the heat of His anger. Yet, Jesus knew exactly what He was doing.

I guess the point I'm trying to make here is that it's okay to use your own judgment. Be honest in the way you release your emotions and dispense punishment. Yes, we must learn a healthy amount of self-control. But most of us do not become violent and abusive when dealing with a child. If you have a problem in that area, you need professional help.

Finally, I would encourage you to be honest with another emotion as well. Be understanding enough to say "I'm sorry" if you find you overreacted or acted in error.

Children Are Not Naughty; Actions Are Naughty

Another ideal theory for parents goes something like this: "I must not attack the child, only the action." For example, a "good" mother would say (calmly), "Darling, I know how much you like snakes, and although boa constrictors make lovely pets, it disturbs me that you've chosen to adorn our home with one."

One should refrain from screaming, "Get that snake out of this house before I call pest control to get rid of both of you!"

Perhaps you're wondering why I placed these child-rearing theories in the mythical-thinking category. After all, they are valid and should be incorporated into child rearing whenever possible. While neither of these theories is wrong, life just isn't quite that simple. The theories leave little room for honest emotion.

No matter how hard we try to live by the rules the experts have laid down for us, we will at times let our emotions rule. Then, not only do we feel guilty for losing control, but we also feel like kids caught playing hooky from school because we failed to follow orders.

What so many of the experts fail to tell us is that, while we can benefit from their advice, it's practically impossible to parent strictly by the book(s)—especially when your kids haven't read them.

Only Animals Have Instincts?

Somewhere along the line child psychologists must have decided mothers had about as much common sense as God gave a goose. Experts have given us detailed and dia-grammed advice on everything, including which end of the baby to diaper.

Mothers are born with instincts for child care, but many of us are so confused with conflicting advice we're afraid to feed the baby without consulting the book.

This is not a suggestion to ban child-rearing books. There is nothing wrong with bringing up baby by the book, pro-viding you use a different book for each child.

Seriously, books that explain how babies grow can be very helpful in answering questions you have about your growing child. In the back of this book, you'll find a reading list of other helpful publications.

My concern is that you not become so confused in the "ought to's" of child rearing that you lose all sense of direc-tion. I've known moms who became so full of conflicting information they didn't know which way to turn, so they actu-ally abandoned their children.

Others ignore the problem. And who could blame a mom for letting the kids run wild? I mean, once you start wading through the options, you could end up drowning. The secret is to glean information you can use and to value your own opinion.

Don't be afraid to use maternal instincts in bringing up your children. More often than not, your own instincts are right and should be used. After all—stop me if I'm wrong—didn't God create those instincts (or spiritual discernments) in us?

Real Mothers Don't Get Sick

There is one hard, fast rule in motherhood. Moms cannot be sick. There is no time. And if you did get sick, no one would be able to take care of you, and finally, your kids won't *let* you get sick.

But don't take my word for it. My friend Ellen had an infected tooth. She was spacey from the pain pills that were doing nothing to relieve her agony. She needed rest. In desperation she decided she had to lie down for a while and left her baby and three-year-old, Erin, in the care of her eleven-year-old son, Ted.

Unfortunately, Erin believed in the old adage that real moms don't get sick and bounced around on Mom's bed wanting to play.

Finally Ted, in all his wisdom, pulled the errant child away and said, "Knock it off, Erin. Let Mommy rest so we can have our *real* mom back."

I rest my case.

To Dream the Impossible Dream

The final parenting myth I'd like to deal with here is one that ground my pedestal to dust. I once believed it was possible, with the right combination of love, discipline, and home atmosphere, to rear the ideal child.

As my children grew, I adopted the idea that they couldn't possibly get into serious trouble. Oh, yes, they were entirely capable of mischief, but nothing more serious. Although I didn't go around waving a banner, I proudly stood firm on the belief that "my kids would never . . ."

One day as I drove past a neighbor's on my way home, I spotted a fire truck. Making my way through the commotion, I noticed there had been a fire in the mailbox.

When I got home, I mentioned what I had seen to the kids. "The neighbor said some kids set it. Probably a prank. Honestly," I continued to rave, "I can't imagine what's gotten into kids these days. How could anyone let their kids be so destructive?"

Caryl nodded in agreement.

David said, "Yeah, that was a pretty stupid thing to do."

A couple of days later I'd forgotten the incident. But the police hadn't. What they turned up sent what little there was left of my ideal-parent facade packing.

"The police were by today," I told my son when he arrived home from school. "Seems as though one of your friends admitted to the mailbox fire. Seems you were with him."

"Yeah. We did it," Dave admitted, "but we didn't mean for the mailbox to catch fire. Sherri was acting like a stuck-up brat. We just threw a firecracker in the box to scare her."

"Let me get this straight. Sherri wouldn't pay any attention to you so you set fire to her parents' mailbox?"

"No, we didn't mean for it to catch fire. How were we supposed to know there was a newspaper inside?"

The boys got off with a couple hours of hard labor. They had to repair the mailbox and listen to a lengthy dissertation on the dangers of fire and the seriousness of tampering with mailboxes.

Superman!

I couldn't look my neighbors in the eye for months. I was too busy sweeping the dust from my ideal-parenting pedestal under the carpet.

Like Don Quixote, I had sung the song and held tight to my impossible dream, only to have it turn into a nightmare. It took years before I realized that the American Dream of motherhood and winning the "ideal parent" award was a fairy tale.

I had learned the hard way that real moms do eat baby food and real moms lose control sometimes. Real moms don't play games and pretend to have all the answers.

Before we leave fantasyland, I have one more mythical mom I'd like you to meet. She is all things to all people. She is the superheroine of our time. She is Super Mom.

In the next chapter we'll examine some of the occupational hazards of being a Super Mom, such as the rising cost of flight insurance, or watching your cape disintegrate as you burn out, and worst of all, letting the kids borrow your costume.

4

The Trouble
with Super Moms

"Hi, Mom. What's up?" My son sounded anything but up.

"Not much," I said. "How are you doing?"

"Terrible. Everything's going wrong."

"Oh, I'm sorry. Anything I can do to help?"

"Not really. I just needed to talk to you. I always feel better when I do."

We talked for a while and I promised I'd pray for him. I reminded him he'd been through tougher times. "You're a survivor," I said. "You'll make it."

"I know, Mom. Thanks." After we hung up, I felt better too. He still needed what I could give him as a mom—reassurance and encouragement.

I felt warm all over. He calls every once in a while just to talk. I know it's because I always tried to make time to listen to him when he was younger. It wasn't always that way. For a brief time in my career as a mother I became so wrapped up in being mother/wife/career woman, I hardly had time to listen to anybody. In fact, I tried so hard it's a wonder my family survived. For a while I wasn't sure any of us would.

It's a Bird. It's a Plane. No! It's Super Mom!

One of the offshoots of the feminist movement is the unsinkable Super Mom. She can single-handedly keep her home in perfect order, care for children with the expertise of a child psychologist, and have a career (outside the home, of course), which she's been told makes her an independent, successful woman. She must be a sex siren for hubby, an elegant hostess, and an all-around neat person. But the Super Mom brigade isn't restricted to working moms. Stay-at-home moms are also urged to join. We are all led to believe we can and must be all things to all people.

The Rising Cost of Flight Insurance

Nothing in this life is free. If you want to join the ranks of super-heroines, you have to accept some of the hazards that go along with the job.

Interestingly enough, the women's movement liberated women right into the same trap that put men into midlife crisis. Many more women are now receiving equal pay for equal work, but they are also getting the headaches, the ulcers, and the burnout that go with the modern-day version of success.

The problem is, most of us moms who opted for the Super Mom routine a few years ago couldn't see into the future. We didn't know the call to freedom and equal rights meant we'd be free to indulge in nervous breakdowns and handle our fair share of stress.

Many of us swallowed the old adage "You can do anything you set your mind to." While I don't entirely want to discount that, I must say that some of us mothers have a tendency to overdo.

Anything You Can Do I Can Do Better

I'm one of those perpetual achievers. I used to think there was nothing I couldn't do, except perhaps play quarterback for the NFL. But on my really up days I might have tried it. I'm always after the brass ring or reaching for a star. So when my friends started chanting, "You, too, can be a Super Mom," I believed them.

Confident and eager to meet the challenge, I bought teal blue leotards, hot pink tights, and matching striped leg warmers. I tossed on a cape and jumped into my rented phone booth. (I figured I'd save money and use the same outfit in my aerobics class.)

With the determination of an Olympic competitor, I strove to accomplish all my goals—in one day. *Time is too short,* I told myself. What if a nuclear war started tomorrow? Everything in my life became an urgency.

My days were filled with keeping my home spotless. I sewed clothes for the kids and me, attended school, or worked as a nurse. I volunteered my time as a room mother and dutifully attended parent-teacher meetings. I excelled in gourmet meals, reared my children by the book(s)—and spent *quality* time with them. I served as a supportive wife and lover to my husband (also quality time). In addition, I worked out daily at a health spa to slim down and stay sexy and healthy. When I had time left over, I would work on calligraphy, paintings, or pottery for self-gratification . . . or was that self-preservation?

I started out singing with great zeal such songs as: "I'm a Woman" and ended up singing, "Nobody loves me, everybody hates me. Guess I'll go eat worms."

The Great American Burnout

It was the pits. I mean, how would you feel if your beautiful Super Mom cape suddenly went up in flames as you suffered a massive burnout?

I had failed. And to top it off, with my cape burned beyond repair, I was grounded. My frustration level grew daily. Since Super Moms tend to do everything in a superhuman way, naturally I had to experience super stress. Much of the time I felt like the inside of Mount St. Helens. Pressure built up within me until I felt as if I would explode. Sometimes I did.

Like the time I crawled out of bed and groped my way to the kitchen at 6:30 one morning to fix the children some breakfast. I'd worked till midnight the night before. Sure, I suffered from exhaustion, but I wanted to give my darlings a special treat. Besides, if I didn't cook breakfast, guilt would sock me in like a dense fog.

I cooked eggs, toast, bacon, and hash browns—the works. Caryl made her entrance with a "Yuk, do we have to eat eggs?" David chimed in with, "I wanted my eggs whole, not scrambled."

I don't know how you are in the morning, but before tea, my brain functions at a slightly less than rational level. With unleashed hostility, I yanked a wooden spoon out of the drawer and shook it at them.

"You eat what's put before you. I could still be sleeping, but instead, I'm out here slaving over a hot stove, so you can go to school with a hot breakfast instead of cold cereal." *Cr-a-ck-ck!* The spoon hit the table. Its top half sailed halfway across the kitchen.

I shoved their plates at them and pitched a fork into the sink. I turned, just in time to watch my only large, glass bowl disintegrate into hundreds of free-falling fragments.

A muffled scream forced its way through my tightly set jaw. I closed my eyes and smoldered. *Control yourself,* my brain commanded. My knuckles whitened as I clung to the counter. *Now, take a deep breath,* continued Brain. *Don't let this thing beat you.* Obediently, I breathed deep, opened my eyes, and tried again.

I pushed a milk carton into the fridge and slammed the door. A threatening thud from inside the big, white box told me I still had troubles. I pulled open the door to a milk flood. Milk gushed endlessly from the tipped half-gallon container, drenching my bare feet and kitchen carpet.

Tears poured down my hot, red face. I savagely grabbed for towels and with hostile vengeance beat on the milk-saturated carpet. Cleanup and tears finally subdued my anger. I looked up at two innocent grade-schoolers, who stared, possum-eyed in wonder that a mother could fall to such a devastating display of violence.[1]

Did I have a field day with guilt over that one. It was the worst blowup I'd ever had, but it made me realize I couldn't go on playing Super Mom.

I knew I had a problem and began to ask myself some serious questions. For example: Why am I doing this? What's more important, my family or the things I do for them?

And another thing, if I were to die tonight, what would my kids remember about me? That I could yell louder than any other mother on the block? That they could walk across the kitchen floor without getting their feet stuck on the Kool-Aid they spilled the day before? That I didn't have time for foolish things like playing tag or Monopoly?

No! No! No! "Oh, kids, please remember all those times we sat huddled together in the rocking chair reading *Winnie-the-Pooh* and *Dr. Seuss.* Remember all the times we laughed together? Remember our trip to Disneyland?"

Hey, wait a minute, I told myself. What am I doing? I spent time loving those kids—not always enough, but I wasn't neglecting them. Then what was the problem? Why was I so tired all the time? Why was I so full of emptiness when everyone told me how fulfilled and successful I'd become?

Then it hit me. I was expecting too much of myself. Even with all the showy props—the costume and the songs—I had never been a real superwoman. Underneath the disguise I was just another laboratory mouse, running wild in a circle cage and never getting anywhere. When I enlisted they'd promised me freedom. It was about time I took it. I went AWOL. I jumped out of the cage and decided I had to stop taking my life so seriously.

I began to realize the floors wouldn't rot if they got cleaned only once a week (or month). And, if I didn't catch all the cobwebs one day, they'd still be there the next. And so what if I didn't get all my sewing done? If the world did end tomorrow, we wouldn't have to worry about what to wear. Slowly I began to develop a "que sera, sera" attitude. Gone was the urgent need to push, push, push. I made time for daily walks and tried to be more available to those special people in my life.

It worked. I turned in my charred cape and phone booth. I kept the tights, leotards, and leg warmers—my contract with the health spa wasn't up for another year. I stopped trying to leap over tall piles of laundry in a single bound. I simply waded through the pile—one sweat sock at a time. The laundry got done—eventually. As I lost the desire to be a Super Mom, I lost the tension headaches and stomachaches.

Leaving superstardom behind wasn't easy. Even after all these years I still experience brief relapses when adrenaline surges through my blood. My heart rate accelerates and beats out a Morse code message to my brain: "You can fly! You can fly!"

Fortunately, I recognize the symptoms. When I feel an attack coming on, I counteract the effect by taking a hike, relaxing in a bubble bath, or forcing myself to sit in the hot tub for half an hour. Another trick that never fails is to curl up with a good novel.

Warning: Super Momming May Be Hazardous to Your Kids' Health

Being a Super Mom is not only a dangerous occupation for moms but it can also have a direct effect on babies. I have come to firmly believe that every Super Mom cape issued should carry the warning "Super Momming May Be Hazardous to Your Kids' Health."

Fortunately, I discovered the stability of having the earth beneath my feet early on. I didn't pass the Super Mom trait on to my kids. Many moms haven't been so lucky.

One of the dangers of living in the high-stress, high-tech society is that we often end up pushing those stresses onto our children. There is a fine line that we must walk between striving for excellence in being the best we can be and pushing beyond the limit. Today's mothers are often under tremendous pressure to compete. We compete in the marketplace for grocery specials, for places to park, and for jobs. Recently, moms have begun to place their children in the heat of competition to turn their kids into Super Babies.

A newspaper article reported that more and more mothers are striving to get their children into the best pre-preschools by making reservations before the child is born. One mother, in order to ensure high social status for her two-year-old, hired a limousine to chauffeur her child to school.

Many of today's parents have fallen into the trap set by a few experts on child development. These experts insist there are lessons for everything and children should be plunged into the world of academia the moment they are born. Some moms have even been encouraged to begin lessons while the child is in the womb.

It is not unusual these days to see parents flash cards in front of their seven-day-old so that by the time he's seven months he has mastered simple math. Some Super Baby boosters believe children can read at eleven months.

So what if the average baby's eyes don't fully focus until three months? And what does it matter that a child can't attest to the fact that he's learned to read seven months before he can talk? The important thing is to get that little brain trained while there is still time.

My Baby, the Genius

When you stop to think about it, moms are really suckers for this Super Baby stuff. What mother in the world doesn't feel that her baby is more intelligent, more adorable, more dexterous than any other baby in the world?

Even though superbabies weren't the "in" thing when my David came along, I found myself extolling his virtues. Friends would have to endure baby pictures and bragging such as: "Oh, look, he's only three weeks old and already he's trying to walk." (In actuality, I had him draped over my shoulder for a burp and he was trying to kick my hands out from under his feet.) "Wow, did you see that? He pointed to the Dior label on my blouse and said, 'Duh . . . duh . . . duh.' He can spell." (Never mind the fact that for three days he'd been pointing to everything, including his toes, and saying, "Duh . . . duh . . . duh.")

It wouldn't have taken much to convince me I had a genius on my hands and should begin flashing math and spelling cards immediately—just as soon as I signed up my brilliant toddler in music lessons, where at the advanced age of two he could learn to play his mini-violin.

Today, many mothers have climbed aboard the Super Baby Express, and they've taken baby along for the ride. Baby business is booming as many women run motherhood as they would a corporation.

All Aboard the Super Baby Express

Glenn Doman, known as the grand guru of baby building, has written such classics as *How to Teach Your Baby to Read, Teach Your Baby Math,* and *How to Multiply Your Baby's Intelligence.* Doman claims, "Tiny children believe that it is their job to grow up. They know instinctively that learning is a survival skill. It's adults who want to keep children children; during the period they learn the most, we treat them like chowderheads."[2]

It's true—babies do learn at an early age. But I worry that all this push-and-shove mentality to get them to excel will create the same kinds of stress, frustrations, and feelings of failure that we see in women who strive to be Super Moms. Yes, babies do learn more in their first few years than in the rest of their lifetime, but think about the vast amount of knowledge that has to be absorbed by those "little sponges" in so short a time. They must learn about life and how to survive in it.

Too Much Too Soon?

Realistically, even the best sponges absorb only so much. Are we trying to fill our babies up with too much too soon?

Babies are born with some primitive instincts, such as the rooting and sucking reflex that helps them find food. From the time they are born, babies must learn where food comes from, and more important, how to let someone know they're hungry. They must learn how to ask Mom and Dad to change their diapers and how to get someone to cuddle them. They must determine who's who in this family they've been given.

Babies must learn how to hold on to things and how to let go. They must learn how to speak adult as well as teach their parents how to understand baby talk.

Another interesting thought is that children want to please their parents. They learn rules by watching how their behavior affects Mom and Dad. Good behavior is associated with smiles, hugs, and kisses while no-no's are met with frowns and punishment.

I'm certain you will agree, babies have a lot to learn without the added pressure of flash cards.

Baby Burnout

While love may be the motive for wanting children to excel, the child often considers that the parents' pleasure in him is in direct proportion to his academic performance.

My concerns for the future of these Super Babies are shared by many experts in the field of child development. In fact, psychologist Lee Salk says, "This pressure for high achievement really sets children up for failure. Love should be unconditional where children are concerned; it should not be based on IQ."[3]

According to Dr. Raymond Moore, a noted developmental psychologist, children who are pressed to read at an early age often develop reading problems and, more seriously, sight impairment later.[4] Child educators are seeing more and more children experiencing burnout by the time they hit second or third grade—some even earlier. What would you call it when a six-month-old looks at his flash cards with a quivering bottom lip and crawls off in the opposite direction? Fear? Anxiety? Frustration?

Maybe he's saying, "If you can't love me unless I play your game, then I'm not sure I want to be loved at all."

Can't you see the stressed-out kid rolling down the street in his computerized Super Baby buggy with a sticker on the back that says, I'D RATHER BE SUCKING MY THUMB?

While trying to saturate those "little sponges" with knowledge, parents are filling them with the stresses and strains so prevalent in our hectic, grown-up world. It's bound to cause problems. The development of Super Baby may have been born out of love and desire for the child to have the very best life has to offer. But it may also be born out of the parents' desire to be successful.

This is a success-oriented culture where material wealth and social-ladder climbing has become an obsession. Competition and grooming the "successful" child can take its toll on his or her young, impressionable body. Maybe it's time to count the cost.

Stress-related ailments that used to be exclusive to adults are seen in more and more children. Today we see many children who suffer from abdominal pain, headaches, ulcers, depression, and a general tiredness or lack of vitality. These sound like the symptoms of a man or woman who's suffering from burnout—not a two-, three-, or four-year-old child.

Perhaps it's time to relax. Maybe we should let children be children and not force them into adulthood too soon. I'd just as soon let the child become an adult naturally. There really is so little time for play. Let's enjoy our children while we can.

Now, let's leave the world of superheroines and mythical, magical moms behind and move forward into part 2. There we'll find the keys that open the doors to what kids need most in a mom.

The Treasures of a Mother's Heart

The world is full of riches, but none of them can compare with the treasures that lie within a mother's heart.

Imagine your motherly heart as a large mansion. As we wander through the corridors we see many doors. Each room contains a wealth of information that can lead to better mothering. Behind one door lies the secret of communication, behind another are rare antiques from the storehouse of our memories, and yet another room is filled with the sound of laughter.

The greatest thing about all these treasures is that they are free. God has given us the keys. Now all we have to do is use them.

As we move along through the chambers of our mansion, let's try the first key on the door marked *Time*.

5

If Time Were Diamonds

The door opens easily. Sunlight scatters shimmering prisms of color through the room. Can you see them? Millions of sparkling diamonds suspended in time.

I hear the ticking of a clock. With each ticktock, a diamond disappears. I watch, powerless to interfere. Helplessness, anger, and regret battle in my mind. "Stop!" I cry. But nothing stops. The diamonds, seconds in time, melt silently away, fading swift and sure into memories.

Turn Around and She's Grown

I think of my children and how quickly they've grown. I remember an incident soon after my youngest left home. It was dark outside. The dim lamp cast quiet shadows across the floor. I was sitting on my nineteen-year-old daughter's empty bed. Caryl had telephoned a few minutes before from California.

"Mom!" Her voice bubbled with excitement. "Guess what?"

"What?" I asked hesitantly. Excitement wasn't unusual for her. She delighted over so many things, but this time I had a

. . . feeling. My intuition told me she was about to announce something I didn't want to hear.

"Mom, we're getting married. Isn't that great?"

"M-m-arried?" A lump the size of a baseball lodged itself in my throat, blocking my words. Her boyfriend seemed like a nice boy, but . . .

"Mom?" The excitement had turned to disappointment. "I wanted you to be happy for me."

Shame on you, I scolded myself. *Even if you don't like the idea, you could at least fake it. Be happy for her. She needs that. Isn't that what a mother is for?* No, I decided. I couldn't lie about how I felt. I never had before. "I-I'm sorry, honey." I managed to squeeze the words through my throat. "It's just such a surprise. I . . . you're so young."

"But we love each other, Mom. And you were my age when you met Dad."

That was different, I wanted to say. But I didn't. "When are you getting . . . married?" I was finding it more and more difficult to talk. *Where had I put the Kleenex?*

"We haven't set a date. Mom, you're not crying, are you? I want you to be happy."

"I can't (sniff) right now. Maybe in a day or two, when I've had a chance to think about it. I really want what's best for you. I love you so much . . . oh, honey, wait a little while. Marriage is a lifetime thing. Please don't rush. It takes a long time to plan a wedding."

"I know, Mom. I love you too. And I *am* sure. We've talked about commitment and we both feel very strongly that marriage should last forever. But I'll think about what you said."

"That's good, honey."

"You know what? We've already decided, we want two boys—"

"What? Don't you think you should get married before you plan a family?"

"Oh, don't worry, we're not . . . besides, we want to finish school first."

"Good idea. I haven't quite gotten used to the idea of marriage yet. I'm not sure you're ready for that, let alone mothering. I'll love being a grandma, but I can wait."

"I know, Mom. Well, I'd better go. I don't want to run the phone bill up too high."

"Right. Well, thanks for calling. I love you."

"Love you too . . . Mom? Please be happy for me."

"I'll work on it."

Be happy, she'd said. Well, I found it very hard to be happy about losing my baby. Oh, I know, she's all grown up. And I knew this day would come. It's just that there were so many things I hadn't taught her yet. I didn't really want her to get married. If I'd called her back and said, "I absolutely forbid it," I wonder what she'd have done? I know what I'd have done at nineteen. I'd have gotten married anyway. She's a lot like me—strong-willed and persistent, in a quiet sort of way.

No, that wasn't the answer. She'd only resent me. I'd worked so hard to keep the lines of communication open—why close them now? I simply had to let her know how I felt, and pray she made the right decision. She'd been making decisions for a long time.

Time . . . I wish there'd been more.

Only Yesterday

I reached for the photo album on the nightstand and opened it, remembering . . .

Caryl always did have a mind of her own—even before she was born. It took her two weeks past the due date before she finally decided to be born. I had labor pains for two hours every day. They just kept getting closer and closer together until the last day, then *boom*—five minutes apart. And do you think she could come into the world like everyone else? No way. My Caryl came out backwards—bottom first.

"What a scrawny little kid," I chuckled as I gazed at the first picture we ever took of her. Her long, skinny legs pointed straight into the air like a ballerina. We used to tease her when she got older.

"Caryl," I would say, "you came folded in half and for days you refused to straighten out. In fact, you were so insistent that when I pulled your legs down, your head would pop up." She grew straight and tall, but she can still fold herself in half.

Then there was the day she came home from the hospital, when she gave her brother his first lesson in sex education.

I had brought the dressing table into the kitchen so I could give Caryl a bath near the sink. David, then nearly two, naturally curious and already in love with his little sister, climbed up on a chair to watch.

As I removed her diaper, I heard a gasp. I looked down. David's mouth hung open and his huge sky blue eyes looked, unbelievingly, at his sister and then at me.

"Mom!" He pointed at his sister's bottom. "Oh, Mom. Poor Caryl. It's gone."

His look of genuine concern kept me from doubling over in laughter. I held myself in check and explained. "It's okay, honey. Girls aren't supposed to have one. Mommy doesn't either."

He cocked his head and looked again at his sister and at me and said, "Oh." With that he scrambled down from the chair and ran off to the living room to play.

As I said before, the kid did things her own way. At two, she came up beside me and tugged at my slacks. "Mommy, I don't want to go potty in my pants anymore." With that announcement, she was completely potty trained.

"It seems like only yesterday," I said aloud. "Now she's all grown up, and just like that she announces she's getting married. Sometimes this business of mothering hurts." I reached for the nearly empty box of Kleenex and blew my nose again.

Time. There's nothing we can do to stop it. But there are some things we can do as mothers to make certain we get full value out of what we have left.

Is Quality Time Enough?

There's no doubt about it—mothering takes time. I wrote in an earlier chapter, a mother doesn't have to be with her children every moment, yet there is a fact we must face—if we don't spend time with our children, how are they going to learn from us?

Every mother, from the moment of her child's entry into the world, must face the question, "How much time will I give to mothering my child?" Or "How much time can I give . . . ?"

Or perhaps a better question might be, "When and how much do they need me?" We will want to devote as much as possible to them, especially in their earlier years . . . and, during their school years . . . and, of course, during their teen years.

Over half of the mothers in this country work outside the home. With the surge of mothers leaving the home there came a controversy between quality time versus quantity time. Some say that you can spend very small amounts of time with your child as long as it is quality time.

For a while I believed that, but I came to see quality time as a rationalization. What better way to talk myself out of feeling guilty when I should have been spending more time with the kids? For me, quality time wasn't enough.

Quality time is important, as most working mothers will agree, but it can hardly be planned. Do you have any idea what happens to a mother who decides that today she and her child will have four quality hours together?

That's the time it rains on your parade. You've planned the perfect outing and your kids tell you of their plans (made months ago) to go roller-skating with friends. Or perhaps it's the time your mother calls to tell you Uncle Clancy is having open heart surgery and would you be a dear and take her to the hospital and wait with her.

Quality Time versus Super Pickle

Say you do manage to gather up your child. One day my friend Kate decided to take her three-year-old, Charlie, shopping with her. It would be a perfect opportunity to spend quality time in meaningful communication.

Kate and Charlie were doing fine. Charlie was laughing and the two were really enjoying each other's company. Suddenly, Charlie let loose with a bloodcurdling scream. Someone had forgotten to tell Kate that it was National Pickle Week and some pickle company had sent out pickle people to market their wares.

A six-foot green pickle, complete with warts, approached Kate and her son, who became hysterical and tried to make a quick exit over Kate's head. "There, now, I won't hurt you," Super Pickle crooned in an attempt to comfort the kid. Charlie, however, refused to be consoled by a talking pickle and screamed louder.

"I'm just going to give your mommy a sample of our crisp, delicious dills." The pickle dismissed their obvious rejection.

"Look, Mr.—I really don't think you should talk to him," Kate managed a muffled reply as Charlie grabbed her face. "He's not used to six-foot pickles."

"Oh, but they're fantastic—"

"I'm sorry, I really have to go."

"Here, just try one." As the green arm shot toward Charlie and Kate, the screams grew in intensity.

Nerves jangled, ears ringing, Kate finally stomped her foot and turned to face the green invader. "I don't want your crummy pickles!" she yelled.

"But they really are quite delicious."

"Shove them in your ear, buster!" Kate's assertiveness finally convinced Super Pickle to back off, but the damage had been done. Charlie was into a full-blown tantrum and couldn't stop.

Kate hurried through the aisles, red-faced, sweaty, nerves demolished. So much for quality time.

While your attempts at spending quality time may not turn out quite so disastrous as Kate's, more often than not it doesn't pay to plan for those times. Besides, this kind of pre-meditated plot tends to keep a parent's eyes focused on the time, not on the child. Special moments with a child come at the oddest moments, and the best way to capture them is to relax and let them happen.

Sometimes quality time comes when your mind is focused in an entirely different direction.

For example, one day when the children were small, I was lying on the grass in the park, reading a novel. They were busily playing on the slides and swings. My youngest came over and plopped down beside me. She was only four then. In her hand she held a dandelion bouquet picked just for me. "Oh, how pretty," I said as I laid my book aside.

"Mommy." She sprawled on her tummy and snuggled beside me. "What makes flowers grow?"

Quality time can seldom be planned. Special moments are like seeds. They must be planted and watered before you can expect them to grow. Then be ready to stop and enjoy the flowers—when they come.

A Poison in Time

There is a phenomenon in our society that seems to be moving at a faster and faster pace. It leaves us with fewer hours every day. At times I wonder if it is part of a conspiracy to destroy us. It is a lethal poison, designed to keep us too busy to enjoy our portion of time.

As a young mother, I drank the sweet potion. I found it gift wrapped in the pocket of my Super Mom costume. It came in a small white bottle labeled *Success*. With one sip, my world began to turn faster and faster, and I was powerless to stop it. Like the March Hare in *Alice in Wonderland* I was caught up in the dizzying merry-go-round of busyness.

Like the hare, my days were an endless flutter of scurrying in and out of meetings, singing, "I'm late, I'm late, for a very important date. No time to say hello, good-bye. I'm late, I'm late, I'm late."

Many well-meaning moms have swallowed this poison. They whirl about their tasks like mini-tornadoes while the poison erodes the time they might have had with their children or husbands, or with God.

My friend Jean Lush tells about a time when she had taken a near-lethal dose:

Years ago, I was running crazy in extreme busyness. I had under my control forty-five teenagers. My three children and my husband and I all lived in a big dormitory.

This was my first introduction to America (having come from Australia). I was a little nervous about the responsibility in the first place. To make matters worse, these were pretty confused kids and they needed a lot of my time.

I would try to spend a certain amount of time with my children, especially the youngest, who was about nine then. Every day we'd eat breakfast together. Every night at bedtime I'd dash from the big girls in the dorm to my youngest child's room. I wanted to make certain I was with her to tuck her into bed.

One night I heard a rumor that an absolute rebellion was going to take place all over the dormitory. I was tense with worry as I had some real characters in that bunch.

Anyway, I looked at my clock and it was half-past eight, so I hurried up to my own little girl's bedroom. We had developed this little bedtime routine. Usually I'd walk in quietly, sit on the side of the bed, and say something calm like, "Well, how's your day been?" Then we would have a leisurely time with a story and prayer. We normally had about twenty minutes to half an hour.

That evening, however, I was anything but calm. I dashed into the room and said, "Heather, are you ready for bed? Have you brushed your teeth? Are your shoes ready for tomorrow? . . ." I looked around with my mouth still running nonstop, "You've done your homework . . . yes. Okay, dear, jump into bed . . . there's a good girl. Hurry up . . . Mummy's only got a few minutes, you see. . . ."

The child looked at me in horror. (Of course she had no way of knowing the pressure I was under or that I'd be on duty all night.)

"Something wrong?" I asked, hoping to goodness nothing was wrong. All I needed was more trouble. When she didn't answer I asked again, "Is something wrong here, Heather?"

She sat on the edge of the bed and refused to get in.

I glanced at my watch and hurriedly said, "All right, dear. Mother's got five more minutes. Now you tell Mum what's the matter."

She didn't answer.

"Come now. Pour all your feelings out, dear. I want it fast."

With that, Heather got into bed in absolute silence. I knew I was dealing with a real passive-resistant child when she said, "Nothing," and turned her face to the wall.

Well, now I knew something really was wrong. "Oh, no." I looked at my watch again. "Dash it all, only three minutes." I breathed deeply, bent over the bed, and turned her over to face me. "Come now, dear, tell Mother. Is something wrong?"

"Mummy—Mummy, sit down."

So I sat stiffly on the edge of the bed, thinking, *Oh, dear, I've got to get back to the dorm. I do wish she'd hurry up.* "Okay, dear, now tell Mother what's the matter."

"Mummy, I can't talk to you like this. Why don't you lie down?"

Well, our five minutes were up now, so in desperation I flattened out on the bed, every inch of me stiff with mounting tension.

"Mummy, I can't talk to you like that!"

"Oh, dear, why not? I'm lying down like you said, right on the bed here, so please get a move on."

"Mummy," she said. "Lie down in your soul."[1]

Does your hectic life make you rush through moments made for children? Has busyness poisoned your time? Do you look back and realize that vast spaces of time have disappeared before your eyes?

The next time you are tempted to hurry through a bedtime or other special moments reserved for the kids, take a deep breath and "lie down in your soul."

Try the Antidote

I'm certain there are many mothers who would love to lie down in their souls but can't. Perhaps the poison has become too strong. But there is an antidote. The cure is called patience, and while results may not be fast, they are sure.

Patience is something all mothers are potentially equipped with. As a young child, I had more patience than was ordinarily allotted to humans. At the age of six I could patiently move dust around on one piece of furniture for hours. Mother would find my patient streak rather annoying—and all because I could take a whole morning with a task that she could have done in half an hour.

As I grew older, my patience stayed with me. At the age of twelve, I could patiently slip out of the house, find my favorite reading tree, and devour a Trixie Belden or Nancy Drew novel in two or three hours. Then I would patiently wander back to the house and get to the chores my mother had asked me to do before I left the house. (On my lucky days Mom would have gotten impatient and done the chores herself.)

Most of the time I was not so lucky. Usually I meandered in, she'd stand, hands on her hips, and yell, "Where have you been all day? I told you to get the vacuuming done *before* you went out to play." Honestly, sometimes my mother had no patience at all.

When I began to rear children of my own, my patience waned. It wasn't just the children, it was the way we lived. I had already tasted the poison mislabeled *Success*. In our society, if you don't hop on the treadmill and start running, you lose—or so I was led to believe. Before long, my patience bottomed out. In fact, if it had been listed as a commodity in the stock market, my drop in patience would have caused another major depression.

When patience deserted me, it was replaced by stress and anxiety. A sense of urgency overtook the calm spirit I once had. Too often I found myself balling my hands into fists and wanting immediate solutions to all my problems. The only thing that would have made matters better was a thirty-six-hour day. What a mess. I was planting seeds of impatience and seeing them take root in my kids.

For example, I could see impatience growing in my son when he

wanted to sleep on top of his bedspread, in his clothes, so he wouldn't have to make the bed or get dressed before school the next day.

risked falling down the stairs carrying three sacks of groceries so he wouldn't have to make two trips.

ran away from home at sixteen because we weren't treating him like a man and letting him stay out as late as he wanted.

I needed to get my patience back. Patience is listed in the Bible as a fruit of the Spirit. I knew it was one of the things God would give me if I asked. So I did. I took a bite of the patience fruit and have been improving ever since.

If you're a mother who, like me, cries out to God, "Lord, give me patience . . . and I want it right now," here are a few suggestions to help you find it:

Pray. Ask God to instill the fruit of patience in you.

Affirm. Habits can be hard to break, and chances are, your conversion from busy bee to patient saint will not occur overnight. In fact, there may always be a temptation to let anxiety and stress take over. Even if patience evades you, be patient.

God promises to give us the desires of our hearts. Keep affirming the change with phrases such as: "I am slowing down," or "I am becoming a patient person." Affirm yourself every day.

Teamwork. Tell your family about the plan to develop more patience. Chances are, they'll all agree. Oh, not that you're the only one who needs more, but that they could use more too. If you check it out, you may find your children have taken a few nips of the busyness poison as well. Pray for each other. Remind each other in a gentle or laughing way.

Imitate the Master of Patience, Jesus. Learn all you can about Him and from Him.

Exercise your faith. Visualize Jesus cleansing you of the toxins against time: busyness and impatience. See Him transfusing you with tranquillity as He feeds you with the fruit of the Spirit.

Nurture the seed of patience growing inside you. Water it with your desire to rest in the Lord. Feed it with God's Word and faith and watch it grow. Don't slow the process by trying to hurry it along. Just relax and let it happen.

Trust that God will build in you the patience you seek.

There are other ways to neutralize the poisons against time. As you pass through other doors you'll find them. There are love, making memories, listening, and forgiveness. There are many ways to heal but there is no way to bring back the past.

Children grow so fast. Spend time with them. Perhaps the greatest lesson I've learned about time is that before I spend it, I'd better count the cost. I've expressed my feelings in this poem.

If time were diamonds . . .
would I gather each precious moment to my breast?
And when they fade would I mourn and wish them back?
Or would I simply sigh—thankful for memories,
And move on to the next,
Knowing I had done my best.

6

A Room Full of Memories

Let's move down the corridor of our mansion to where the diamond dust of time settles. This deep, rich mahogany door creaks with age as it swings open to welcome us. Billowy priscilla curtains grace the windows. It is a room filled with memories. Walls are lined with portraits of ancestors long dead but often remembered.

The room houses antiques, relics that tie the past to the present. It holds different memories for each of us. This chapter is a lure to cast you into the past to gather special memories—a heritage for your children. It is also to encourage you to begin a room full of memories for your children.

I will share some memories out of our family's past. As I do, think about your own. Write down the thoughts that come to you, and as you do, your memory room will begin to fill with a treasure more valuable than any gem—your family—your heritage.

In one corner sits an ancient Singer sewing machine. Remember how Great-Grandma used to pump the pedal and make it whir? A velvet-covered photo album, its pages yellow with age, catches my eye. I blow away the dust and watch a billion golden specks dance upon the sunbeams.

Here's an antique RCA Victrola that belonged to Great-Great-Grandma Stephens. "She's gone now," I tell my son when he sees the picture of himself as a baby lying in the old woman's arms. But we have that five-generation picture.

Leaning against the big woodstove is a cast-iron skillet. Remember the time Great-Grandma Cora caught the nanny goat eating Granddad's long johns? She grabbed the first thing she could get her hands on, this skillet, and chased the old goat clear across the pasture.

Great-Grandma Cora never liked that goat. Can't say I blame her—especially after it sneaked in the back door and jumped on the dining-room table she'd just set.

Memories Tell Us Who We Are

I've often felt that one of the greatest gifts I could give my children was to pass along a rich heritage. I want them to know their ancestors and where they came from. Kids need a mom to show them that they can play an important part in the history of a family. Many families have developed a family tree. If you don't have one, you may want to start one to go in the front of a memory journal.

Our family tree is filled with interesting people. My father was born in Sweden and sailed to America in 1928 at the age of eighteen. My mother was born in a farming community in North Dakota. Her parents were pure-blooded Norwegians who came over about 1909. We are not royalty, just Scandinavian and proud of it.

My husband is a mixture of German, Scotch-Irish, English, and one one-hundred-twenty-eighth Indian. His great-granddad and grandma participated in the Cherokee Land Rush. Later they headed west to the Oregon territory.

His grandmother's family are descendants of the Fairbanks family—one of the first to settle in the colonies. They sailed from England on the *Griffin,* a year after the *Mayflower,* and built the Fairbanks house in Dedham, Massachusetts, the oldest frame house still standing in the United States.

The children's grandfather was stationed at Pearl Harbor during the Japanese attack on December 7, 1941. Grandpa Gene helped beach the battleship *Nevada,* after it had been bombed, to keep it from sinking and blocking the channel. Grandpa's brother, Harvey, was killed in the same bombing.

My children are part of a colorful history. Children are interested in their background. My kids always used to ask me questions like, "Did they have cars when you were a kid, Mom?" It is exciting for them to see their names on the family tree. Memories tell us who we are.

It takes time to build those memories. One nice thing about sharing memories is that moms don't have to tell all the tales alone. In fact, sometimes it's more effective when Grandpa, Grandma, or Great-Aunt Flo do the honors. Gloria Gaither and Shirley Dobson in their book *Let's Make a Memory* suggest a prearranged visit to be made with grandparents and/or great-grandparents (or uncles and aunts) for the purpose of recording family history.

I Remember Mama

When your children are grown, what would you like them to remember about you? There are several ways you can have a hand in what memories they hold on to. Building memories is one of the nicest things you can do for your children and yourself.

We can't control all the memories our kids keep, but we sure can help make the ones that count. For a start, think back to what you remember most about your childhood.

I remember . . . riding in the front seat of my parents' old Model T. I would stand between Mom and Dad, and we'd sing a rousing chorus of "Yo ho ho, you and me. Little brown jug, how I love thee."

You might wonder what they were doing teaching me, their sweet, innocent baby, songs like that, but I never thought about the words . . . only the love. In fact, I didn't even realize what those words meant until just now as I wrote them down.

I remember . . . Mama baking bread and fixing me a thick slice with fresh cream and homemade jelly. And Mama playing her guitar, teaching us to sing along.

I remember . . . standing out in the backyard with my dad. He was visiting for the day. Dad suffered from tuberculosis and had to stay in a TB sanitarium. We'd had turkey for dinner. Funny—I don't remember much about the meal . . . only the love. He made a wish with me and we each pulled on an end of the wishbone until it broke. I won. He said we had to bury it so the wish could come true and I wasn't to tell anyone. I didn't. I had wished he'd get well and come home. Several months later, he did.

I remember . . . jumping into the big double bed where Grandma and Grandpa Olsen slept, early, early on cold winter mornings. I'd snuggle down between the two of them and hug them awake. I don't remember much about what we said . . . only the love.

How will your children remember Mama? Often, it's not simply the things a person *does* that make a memory dear, but the way a person *is*. For example, when I remember family members, I first remember what they were like. Were they grumpy and complaining, or were they fun-loving? Did they seem to want time to pass quickly so death could alleviate their misery, or did they savor each moment as though it were the last?

One of the ways to develop good memories for your children is to learn the art of celebrating life.

Life Is a Celebration

If an occasion is worth celebrating it is worth celebrating because God made it so. Whether it is birth, life, love, marriage, graduation, death, national integrity, material plenty, or spiritual salvation that we are celebrating—it is a gift of God. Celebrate in such a way as never to offend the Giver![1]

Eugenia Smith-Durland

Have you ever thought of mothering our children as one of life's celebrations? We celebrate birthdays, holidays, and the Fourth of July, but life is more than an occasional splash in the pool of existence.

As a mother who wanted the best for her kids, I felt it important to teach them how to celebrate something more than Christmas. I wanted them to:

Celebrate . . . the victory of a turtle in a race against time. Or Dr. Seuss's green eggs and ham.

Celebrate . . . the opening of a robin's egg as the scrawny, near-skeletal creature announces its arrival.

Celebrate . . . as we watch a caterpillar spin itself into a tomb and rise again as a colorful, winged creature—free to fly.

Celebrate . . . as we listen and feel the heartbeat of a baby in Mom's belly.

Celebrate . . . and be like the sun, bursting forth in a fireworks display announcing its glorious coming. It warms the day and gives freely of its light. Then when the day's work is over, it settles down in a brilliance not easily forgotten. Even when clouds cover the sun, it is still there—shiny and warm, ready to seep into us and cheer us when the clouds pass.

An advertisement for General Foods International encourages you to "celebrate the moments of your life." We don't need the coffee, however, to help us celebrate. We can simply tap the resources inside us.

We live such busy lives. How many celebrations pass by unnoticed in yours? In all the children I have questioned about what they needed most in a mom, none of them ever said, "I need a mom who will show me how to celebrate life and take pleasure in each moment of the day."

But now that my children are older, it's those mini-celebrations they remember best.

The Making of a Memory

Memories and celebrations are wonderful, but how can we hold on to those memories? The mind can hold a vast storehouse of information, but it's amazing how easily we forget. Below I've listed a few ideas that we've used to keep memories in our home.

Pictures. When our children were young we took pictures of everything. We captured all the intimate details of the first bath, the first *goo,* the first tooth, and even when they mastered potty training. We have pictures of each Christmas and Easter, of camping trips and picnics. We snapped pictures of each acrobatic trick from the time they learned to balance on the palm of Daddy's hand (at around the age of one) through their gymnastic meets in grade school and junior high.

The pictures are available to the kids anytime. I remember one evening hearing the downstairs den exploding with laughter. My kids, then in high school, had pulled out the slide projector and were showing slides to their friends.

Repetition. We repeatedly spent time with the children. We made a point of spending time together as a family. The children remember, because we made a habit of enjoying life. We bought a tent trailer when the children were young and went camping nearly every weekend during the summer. Naturally, we took pictures that now help to jog our memories and remind us of the fun we had.

A friend tells us how she made a habit of taking a walk with each child separately on a regular basis. These were special times of sharing secrets and talking in depth.

Another friend, Angela, shared this:

There are seven kids in my family and I'm the oldest. I had to pick up a lot of slack for my mom. Looking back, I have a hard time remembering her doing anything with me alone, except for this: Every once in a while, she would take me out on a long walk.

We would go around the suburbs for about an hour. We were alone. I don't remember her reading to me or anything in particular, but I remember those walks.

That's why it's so important for me to spend time with my kids. I saw a poem in a catalog once that included this line: "I wish I'd found the time to do the little things you asked me to."

Perhaps that's the lament of every mother. I don't know, because my kids are small yet. Nevertheless, I try to do something with them alone every day. Sometimes it's just reading with them before bed. I take walks with my kids, too. Being outdoors does something for us.

Ultimately, I hope my children will remember that I showed them I loved them in many ways, one of which was time alone with them.

Tradition. Especially during the holidays, tradition helps to build and store memories. We try to keep the traditions brought over to this country from our ancestors' homeland. Mine are from Sweden and Norway, and our yuletide wouldn't be complete without a proper Scandinavian food fair of *lefse, fattiman,* and *krumkake,* just to name a few.

Every year, a week or so before Christmas, we would join our longtime friends on a Christmas tree hunt up in the mountains. Our two families stopped at a park on the way and ate a snack and warmed up with hot chocolate. Then we made our way up into the snowy fields and searched for the perfect tree. Most of the time, our trees were never as thick or well-shaped as the kind that were groomed for such occasions. But they were special, because we braved the elements and tracked them down in the wilderness, as our ancestors might have.

Our trees were never elegantly ornamented with color-coordinated balls and glitter either. They held our handmade ornaments, and every year the boughs seem more endowed. I still have many ornaments the children made and proudly display them.

Spontaneity. Not all memories of the holiday times need to be based on tradition. Sometimes spontaneity builds the best memories of all. One Christmas the kids decided, on the spur of the moment, to dress in Mary and Joseph costumes. With a doll playing the part of Jesus in swaddling clothes, they gave us their unedited version of the Christmas story. We took pictures to preserve the memory.

Journals. One sure way of storing memories, besides photos and the closets of your mind, is a journal in which you write those special events you want to remember. Memories, if left to the imagination, often fade. It is a special treat to spend a rainy day rummaging through photos and journals of days gone by.

Often, as children grow older, especially during their teens, we may forget those happy family moments for a while. My son had an especially stormy adolescence. There were times when I wondered if we'd ever have a happy memory again. But we have. Even then we found that memories were a way to bring back smiles. As your family grows, keep your memories, ponder them in your heart, and share them from time to time in family gatherings.

Play the "Remember When" game when your family gets together. Just remind the kids of something they once did, like, "Hey, remember when you operated on that fat snake to see what was inside and delivered its baby?"

"Remember when?"

Memories Can't Take the Place of People

No matter how sweet the memories, it's important that we be there for our kids whenever possible.

I remember a TV show where Punky Brewster, a fourth-grader, was given an assignment by her teacher to make a family tree. Punky couldn't do it—she had no family.

She lived with a foster father after her mother had apparently deserted her. That evening as her foster father tucked her into bed, Punky said, "I miss my mommy so much."

"Yes, but you still have memories."

"I know." Punky sighed. "But you can't talk to a memory. You can't hug or kiss a memory. You can't sit on a memory's lap. Memories don't even have laps."

Building memories is wonderful, but memories can never take the place of a mother's presence. Kids need a mother who takes time to be in the present to build memories for their future's past.

Memories are all we have left of the time that slips away. Perhaps the greatest hindrance to making memories with your children is the idea that you can always do it tomorrow. I don't want to be a pessimist, but we really don't know how many tomorrows we have left, or what they hold. So start building memories today.

7

In the Heart of a Stone

As we close the door to our past and move down the corridor, we come to our third door. The key fits easily, but when we try to push the door open, we meet with resistance. Come on, push. Harder! It's moving—just enough to let us squeeze inside. As we step into the room we find dozens of rocks and boulders scattered across the floor and pressed against the door. No wonder it was so hard to open.

Perhaps you're puzzled and are tempted to ask, "A pile of rocks? What value could these have?"

I asked that myself when I entered this room for the first time. I stooped to pick up a small rock the size of a grapefruit and turned it in my hand. So dull and drab, yet it appealed to my sense of adventure. I had heard of rocks called thunder eggs that held within their dull, thick, gray walls a breathtaking crystalline quartz.

Curious, I picked up a hammer and chisel from a long wooden table, stained with age and gouged by a rock hound's tools. I worked at the stone, my concentration intense. Finally my tapping was rewarded—the stone broke. I set down my tools and gazed in awe at the sight.

Hundreds of miniature pinnacles rose to meet the light, like the Grand Canyon or an ice cave carved in crystal. Lavender, pink, and silver reflections shimmered in the light, casting rainbows across the drab gray walls.

In this room lies the answer to better communication between mother and child. For a parent, sometimes communication can be as hard as splitting rock. But with persistence, and using the tools of patient talking and listening, you can break through the sometimes uninteresting or crusty surface. Once inside, you will find a treasure of words and ideas more brilliant and rewarding than the most valuable stone.

Communication is like a marriage. There are two parts that must come together to make a whole. There must be a balance on both parts for communication to work effectively. So often, we let words fall out of our mouths or bounce off our ears without taking the time to really consider what we're saying or hearing. At those times our words are a superficial means of making conversation.

I'd like us to take a look at our first tool—talking.

I'm not going to go into all the ways we talk to people, but I will give you a few examples of ways in which moms communicate with their kids and take a look at the results.

Nag! Nag! Nag!

I've come to believe there is a nag in every woman. But not every woman nags in a detrimental way. In my years as a mother I have learned there are two methods of nagging. One is effective, the other is not.

Nagging, I've discovered, is a matter of attitude. If you continually criticize, browbeat . . . well, take a look at this example.

Ellen, mother of three, felt it was her duty to consistently point out her children's mistakes and get them shaped up.

"For crying out loud, Andy," she would yell after him as he slipped out the door to play with his friends. "Why can't you be more like your sister? I always have to clean up after you and I'm getting tired of it. Do you hear me?"

Andy heard; he just wasn't listening anymore. It was easier to walk away. Even if he kept his room spotless, she would have found something wrong. *Just a few more years,* he told himself, *and I can leave home. Then she won't have to put up with me anymore.*

Andy is a grown man now. His mother still nags. "Why don't you ever call me?" she whines. "Is that any way to treat your own mother?" He visits her once a week as a dutiful son. If not for guilt, he might even stop these visits. She is still disappointed in him. And he, after all these years, still wants to please her, but he can't. He never could.

Ellen is the kind of woman talked about in Proverbs. She is quarrelsome, contentious, and her words are as annoying as a continually dripping faucet (see Prov. 19:13). Her method of communication is negative and one-sided.

If you feel you must nag, go ahead, only shift the emphasis from criticism to encouragement. Remove the frown and add a smile. Do a little less talking and a little more listening. I'll be talking about the art of listening later in this chapter, but first a word on the positive side of nagging.

Creative Nagging 101

In Erma Bombeck's book on motherhood, she dreamed of a fictional class called Creative Nagging 101. Although such a class doesn't exist, it should. Nagging in a creative way can be an excellent tool for mothers in teaching the essential principles of life.

Of course, by now you know I don't mean the senseless, faucet-dripping nagging. I mean words of wisdom repeated regularly to help develop lifelong habits.

Maybe you don't agree, but I ask you, where would you be today if your mother hadn't told you (often), "Always wear clean underwear. You never know when you'll be in an accident and have to go to the hospital." Another great one was, "Never squeeze the toothpaste in the middle and always replace the cap."

Although I haven't been entirely serious about this nagging business, I do see it as beneficial.

Creative nagging (repetition) is important. Bible verses, proverbs, and Christian principles need to be repeated so that, when children are old, they will not depart from the truths they learned at Mother's knee. Rules are better remembered when they are repeated clearly and concisely on a regular basis and at appropriate times.

Creative nagging is a mother's way of saying *I love you*. One friend, Nancy, stopped nagging completely.

"They never listen to me anyway," she rationalized. Nancy stopped telling her teenage son to get his hair cut before she entered him in the Miss America Pageant. She stopped urging her daughter to clean her room by taking down the poster that said, "Cleanliness is next to godliness." When Nancy neglected to tell her ten-year-old to eat her peas at dinner one night, the child burst into tears and cried, "You don't love me anymore!"

Needless to say, Nancy saw the wrong she had done and changed her ways. Now, when her children pretend to ignore her words of wisdom, Nancy smiles. "Someday, when they're older, they'll remember."

So you can see, nagging can be a way of saying to your kids, "I love you, and I care about who you are and what you do." And after all, don't kids need a mother who cares?

Talking Stones

Just as there are two ways of nagging, there are two ways of just plain talking. One is superficial—a how's the weather, drink your milk, how was school kind of conversing. Some people go through their whole lives never going much deeper than the surface. They never reach the delicate and treasure-filled inside layers.

As a mom I always wanted to get inside my kids. I wanted to see the beauty God created within their minds and souls. But I've discovered there's only one way to find that inner treasure. I had to first show them the inside of me.

How? By letting them know how I felt about . . . well, about all kinds of things. They know a part of me that whips out her squirt gun, just to have a little fun. They know a mom who sometimes cries at old movies, weddings, gymnastic meets, and sunsets.

I've been known to share moments out of the past, dreams I've had, or silly things I've done. Sometimes they've been amazed that I've had the same feelings they experience.

They know a mom who more than once made a fool of herself as a teenager. Like the time I pretended to have as my constant companion a six-foot irresistible rabbit. I could never have done it without my best friend, but the two of us were dubbed loonies by our fellow students for months.

Letting your kids see inside you can open the doors of communication. I remember one evening several years ago when my daughter, then a teenager, didn't want to talk to me. She'd come in at 1:00 A.M. Her curfew was 12:00.

"You're late," I said. "And what have you been doing for the last six hours?"

"Nothing." She turned to hang her coat in the closet.

"You spent six hours doing nothing?"

"We went to a movie . . . Mom, you just don't trust me." She threw up her arms and stomped off to her room.

"Try me." I followed.

She sighed. "We pulled into the driveway before 11:00 and . . . started talking."

Now at this point the conversation could have gone several ways. I could have said, "Talking? You sat in a parked car for two hours with the guy and just *talked?*"

That's what I could have said, but accusations would probably have turned her off completely. I'm not going to take credit at this point for being an ideal mother psychologist. More likely, my stroke of genius was accidental because I remembered a time when I'd been unjustly accused of the same thing. What I did say was this:

"Talking, huh?" I grinned and arched an eyebrow. "Hmmmm. That I can believe."

"You can?" She stared at me.

"Sure." I sat on her bed and hugged my knees to my chest. "I remember dating this really cute guy in high school. After he brought me home, we got started talking and couldn't seem to stop. We sat there for two hours. I loved watching his dimples . . . and those eyes."

"Mom!" It was a half-scold and half-giggle. "Do you expect me to believe that all you did was talk?"

"Well . . . he did kiss me once."

"Only once?" Caryl flopped across the bed on her stomach.

"Yeah . . . unfortunately. How about you? Tonight, I mean." She wrinkled her nose. "Twice, but I couldn't get into it."

"Really?"

"Hmmmm. He's nice as a friend, but . . . you know, no sparks."

"I've dated a few of those myself."

"Mom . . ." she hesitated. "Did you ever break curfew?"

"Once. I got grounded for two weeks, and it wasn't even my fault. After a pep rally this guy brought about ten of us home. One of the girls lived way out in the boondocks. Would you believe the car stalled about a mile from her house? A couple of the guys had to go for help. By the time they dropped me off I was forty-five minutes late."

"You mean Grandma and Grandpa grounded you for that? It wasn't your fault."

"Tell me about it. I argued a lot, but they wouldn't budge. I couldn't believe they'd be so mean. But I guess it worked. I never broke the curfew rule again."

"Mom," she turned to me. "Since it upset you so much, and you know how awful it feels, and since I was in the driveway before 12:00, don't you think we could forget about grounding me this once? I promise I won't do it again."

"Not a chance, sweetie. I'm sorry, but I'll have to ground you. Two weeks."

"Rats!"

"I know it's hard, but you broke the rules."

"Oh, I know. It isn't that, it's just . . . well," she looked up at me and gave me a knowing wink. "Too bad he wasn't worth it."

Sometimes, opening yourself can open the lines of communication.

Let's take a look at the second tool used in effective communication. This one might be even more important than talking.

"You Never Listen"

Do you ever get the feeling your children aren't listening to a thing you say? If that's the case, maybe you should take a few minutes to examine why. Few people ever really take the time to listen to others. I mean *really* listen. Perhaps your children are not listening to you because you don't listen to them. Perhaps they can't truly listen because they've never learned how.

Listening is more than just hearing. True listening is loving someone enough to give him or her your full attention.

As parents we are bombarded with books and articles that tell us how to talk to our kids. But not a lot has been written or taught on how to listen.

A part of really loving someone is to give your attention by listening intently to what is said. While children learn to read and write, few of them have been taught to speak and fewer to listen.

M. Scott Peck, in his book *The Road Less Traveled,* says:

> We spend an enormous amount of time listening, most of which we waste, because on the whole most of us listen very poorly . . . we would be wise to give our children some instruction in the process of listening—not so that listening can be made easy but rather that they will understand how difficult it is to listen well. Listening well is an exercise of attention and by necessity hard work. It is because they do not realize this or because they are not willing to do the work that most people do not listen well.[1]

Have you ever gone to a lecture or tuned in to a program in which you were especially interested in the topic and really listened to what was being said? Listening intently for hours or even a few minutes can give a person a tension headache and muscle spasms in the neck. Listening is not just a job for our ears. It's a difficult and time-consuming task that requires full concentration.

I know, because I'm one of the guilty people who has at times been too lazy to listen fully. A conversation with my daughter several years ago brought this important principle into focus for me.

"Mom." Caryl entered the kitchen and plopped herself on a stool near the counter.

"What, honey?" I didn't look at her; I was measuring flour into a bowl. *One cup. Two. . . .*

"Guess what? Marie and I are going to try out for rally squad. Can we practice over here Monday nights?"

"Hmmmm. That's nice." *What did she say, rally squad practice? Oh, did I forget the salt?*

"Mom, can we?"

"Can you what?"

Caryl sighed audibly and wandered into the living room to flip on the television set. "Never mind." I could hear the pout in her voice. "You never listen."

"I'm listening, really I am." *Who am I kidding? How could I have been listening when I can't remember what she said?*

I apologized. She forgave me. I set aside my biscuits, then sat beside her—my hands (and head) empty of other things, and listened.

How many of us grow up never learning how to really listen, because no one ever cared enough to hear what we had to say?

"My dad never listens to me," a thirteen-year-old girl told me. "He pretends to, but how could he be? Before I'm even finished talking he's giving me his opinion. It's as if he's thinking while I'm talking because he has already made up his mind that what I have to say isn't important."

Listening to children, especially younger ones, can be quite a challenge. After all, trying to listen intently to the incessant chatter of a four-year-old could drive you crazy. In some instances it's permitted to only half listen, as long as we are careful not to develop a habit of using the practice all the time.

On the other hand, when we take the time and effort to listen carefully to everything the child is saying to us, we are telling him or her without words, "You are valuable to me. What you say is important."

As you truly listen to your child, you begin to see a unique person who will undoubtedly have some interesting observations. Out of their innocence, children often have great insight and wisdom. We can learn a great deal from them when we work to gain access to their inner core. Listening helps us to know our children better, which will enable us to teach them more effectively. Another side benefit is that when you make the effort to actively listen, your child will most likely listen to you.

"True listening, total concentration on the other," says Dr. Peck, "is always a manifestation of love. An essential part of true listening is the . . . temporary giving up or setting aside of one's own prejudices, frames of references and desires so as to experience as far as possible the speaker's world from the inside, stepping inside his or her shoes."[2]

Through effective communication, we can better love, accept, and understand our kids. By talking and listening intently we can find treasures in our children's minds—like color, crystal, rainbows, and light in the heart of the stone.

8

Weaving in the Threads of Discipline

Still farther down the corridor, we come to a fourth door. Behind it we hear the enchanting strains of Beethoven's "Fuer Elise." A welcoming sun pours lazy gold streams across a hardwood floor. The walls are lined with large spools filled with threads of every color and texture. In the center of the room stands a Swedish four-harness loom.

The loom is threaded and ready for use. There are many predetermined factors—the color, the strength of the warp threads, the texture, and the basic pattern. The Master Weaver has left a set of instructions. If I follow them, having a specific goal, and take the time necessary to weave the threads with patience and accuracy, I can create a nearly flawless cloth. I could, however, choose to weave without pattern or purpose, simply depressing pedals at random in an undisciplined fashion, and hope for some sort of salvageable piece.

Producing a functional weaving is much like rearing a child—it takes the discipline of following a plan and having a purpose. Discipline is a fiber woven into everything we do. Without it our lives would be unbearable. Children need moms who know the importance of discipline in adults as well as in children. God delivers into our hands a baby, not yet finished, needing certain threads woven into his or her life in order to become complete.

A Gift from God

A child is often referred to as a "gift from God." When a mother first holds her tiny infant, there is no doubt her baby was heaven-sent. I, for one, was filled with a sense of awe that God would entrust such a precious life into my hands.

But gifts are ours to keep—children are not. They are really on loan, and one day God comes to collect. I think perhaps the *gift* is in being given the opportunity to take part in the process of weaving the child into an adult. As parents, we are granted the first option. We choose the first threads. Someday others, whether you want them to or not, will come in to insert threads of immorality, greed, arrogance, and disobedience, just to name a few.

We must then weave quickly and with wisdom. We will want to weave in an abundant supply of threads called love, joy, patience, kindness, goodness, faithfulness, gentleness, and self-control. The child's weave should be thick and durable so that when others come with teachings of wickedness, our child will be able to stand strong and well-disciplined against them.

Discipline, the Necessary Thread

The Master Weaver designed a plan in which discipline of His people plays an intricate part. He has woven into all of us a desire for order. He is disciplined and well-ordered and has created us in His image. Consequently when we live unorganized, hectic, and undisciplined lives, we become restless and basically unhappy.

God uses discipline as a way of keeping us on the right track. In Proverbs 22:15 (KJV) we read, "Foolishness is bound in the heart of a child; but the rod of correction shall drive it far from him." Discipline says, "I love you and I care about how you grow." In his book *Dare to Discipline,* James Dobson says:

> Although love is essential to human life, parental responsibility extends far beyond it. . . . Love in the absence of instruction will not produce a child with self-discipline, self-control, and respect for his fellow man. Affection and warmth underlie all mental and physical health, yet they do not eliminate the need for careful training and guidance.[1]

Discipline can be a scary thing for many moms, and it's easy to see why. Nearly everyone you talk to has a different opinion. I have an opinion as well. While I don't claim to have all the answers, I have, over the years, developed some commonsense "rules" you may find helpful:

1. Adopt methods you feel are best for you and your child.
2. Realize that what works for one child won't necessarily work for another.
3. Work for conformity and consistency of discipline methods among all who care for the child.
4. Always discipline with an attitude of love.

Defining Discipline

One of the problems many of us have in the area of discipline is seeing discipline as a necessary evil—something we'd rather not deal with. Consequently, children today are often undisciplined and running scared. A friend told me about a six-year-old child who kept hitting her while she and the child's mother were talking. The mother totally ignored the child's actions. "He was an obnoxious brat," my friend said. "I felt like

I should have done something. But it wasn't really the kid's fault. His mom obviously doesn't know a thing about discipline."

Children need a mother who loves them enough to discipline them wisely. How do we do that? Perhaps one of the first keys to effective discipline is understanding what it actually means. Many tend to use the words *discipline* and *punishment* synonymously. Although chastisement, correction, punishment, and penalize are all captured within its meaning, the word has far deeper implications. To discipline also means to guide, instruct, train, prepare, indoctrinate, develop, moderate, restrain, and correct, to name a few. It implies orderliness, habit, regimen, and adherence to certain rules, as opposed to the chaos, confusion, and disorderliness of the undisciplined.

Effective discipline incorporates forms of punishment as well as methods for teaching and guiding a child toward an orderly and self-disciplined way of life. Discipline is something we do *for* our children, not something we do *to* them. In a devotional I was reading, I came across these words by Hannah Whitall Smith:

> If love sees those it loves going wrong, it must, because it is love, do what it can to save them. Any supposed love that would fail to do this is really selfishness.

No matter what a child's age, effective discipline and love are essential to their physical, emotional, and spiritual well-being. One of the most important parts of discipline is the setting of boundaries.

Even Children Understand the Need for Discipline

Children who control their homes because parents are afraid to or refuse to discipline are miserable tyrants. Though most kids won't admit it, they want and need discipline. When he was about nine years old, my son, David, came to me one day after school with an unusual request. "Mom, I need to study my math, but I can't. Would you make me?"

As part of my research for this book I questioned a number of children about what they needed most in a mom. Here are just two of the responses:

"I need spankings," three-year-old Shelly said in a no-nonsense tone.

"I need my mom to keep me from doing bad things that might hurt me," said Michael, age eight.

I was surprised at how many of the children I questioned spoke of the need for discipline. Even though they may be the first to yell foul when you follow through, they seem to sense that setting boundaries is all part of taking good care of them.

Setting Boundaries

Gregory Bodenhamer says in his book, *Back in Control,* "Children aren't born wanting to obey—or disobey—the rules set down by parents, schools, or society. And one of the greatest stumbling blocks in getting children to behave *properly* is the human desire to do as one pleases."[2]

He goes on to give us what he calls Bodenhamer's Law. "Human beings prefer doing things in their own way, in their own time, and given an option, will sometimes do as they please."

We discipline wisely by establishing and enforcing fair and realistic boundaries. In a book called *Suffer the Children,* author Janet Pais writes:

If children encounter nothing firm in their human environment, they will be confused, anxious, lacking boundaries, lacking a sense of reality. They will not be able to develop as solid, real, sane human beings.[3]

Children need to feel safe and secure, yet have ample space to grow and develop, to experiment and explore the world in which they live. Boundaries tell a child what is acceptable and what is not. Few children today have firm boundaries, and their lives are often full of inconsistencies. It's up to us to provide a structured environment and constant routine whenever possible.

There is more to setting boundaries, however, than drawing a line and saying the child can't cross it. Setting limits entails much more than telling your child "no." While we teach children to respect the boundaries we establish, we also teach them to develop and respect their own.

If this sounds complicated, I don't mean it to be. We can accomplish this business of establishing boundaries for ourselves and one another by simply invoking two timeless principles:

1. Love one another as Christ has loved you.
2. Do unto others as you would have others do unto you.

We bring the principles home by always asking of ourselves and of our children, "Would God want me to do this?" and "Would I want someone to do this to me?" At this point I'd like to recommend a book called *What Would Jesus Do?* edited by Helen Haidle (see the suggested reading list) to help your children with choices. One of the most important aspects of any relationship is knowing where to draw the line.

A Firm Grip and a Flexible Heart

As you develop effective discipline methods, you'll want to remember to keep a firm grip and a flexible heart. Avoid rigidity. Rigor mortis is something that happens to muscles when one has died. It should not happen to our hearts and brains—especially while we're alive.

All too often, in an effort to protect our children or maintain control over them, we may tighten our grip, which often has the opposite effect. Holding too tight can cause resistance. Did I say resistance? Overcontrolled kids, especially if they tend to be defiant, can be like mules—they plant their feet and refuse to budge. Or they run in the opposite direction.

To avoid a conflict of wills consider the following suggestions:

- Let your child know what the rules are and that you are the one in charge. Children need to know what you expect. And until they are well versed in the rules, they need to be reminded of them on a regular basis.
- Make your rules clear and concise. Avoid long, detailed explanations.
- Strive for consensus in disciplining methods used by Mom, Dad, baby-sitters, grandparents, etc. Too many differing thoughts on how to bring up a child can be confusing and chaotic. The Bible tells us that a house divided against itself doesn't stand (Matt. 12:25).
- Scoldings or explanations should be short and to the point (three minutes max).
- Invoke logical consequences. If a child throws a temper tantrum at the toy store, go home without a toy.
- When applicable, expect restitution.
- Be firm, yet flexible. Decide what's really important to you.
- Be consistent. Don't keep changing the rules or the way in which you follow through.
- Don't make idle threats. As one mother aptly put it, "Say what you're going to do and do what you say."
- Don't make unreasonable demands. For example, you wouldn't spank a two-year-old for playing with her food or a four-year-old for wetting the bed.

As you develop your plan for effective discipline, you'll want to decide which behaviors to allow or prohibit. Choose your battles wisely and make certain you can follow through on the limits you set. Be assertive, confident, and consistent. Try not to yell. At a parenting workshop I went to, the speaker wisely stated, "Trying to train children by yelling at them is like trying to drive your car by blowing the horn."

I Try to Be Consistent, But . . .

Most books on child rearing will warn you about the perils of being inconsistent. Some have even stressed that if you don't do anything else, be consistent.

I regret that within my fabric lie a few threads of inconsistency. In fact, there are certain times that I am about as inconsistent as the weather.

For example, one Sunday my son, David (I think he was about ten at the time), had gone to his friend Ryan's house for the afternoon. I called Ryan's home to tell David to come home (we had visitors from out of town). He wasn't there and Ryan's mother didn't know where the boys had gone. (Now I ask you, what kind of mom wouldn't know where her children were? My kind of mom, that's who.)

Naturally, I was upset. David had promised to call if he was going elsewhere. I fretted all day, but no call. Finally, he crashed through the door—on time, his usual exuberant self—and gave me a cheery "Hi, Mom!"

I lit into him. *"Hi!* You've had me worried sick all afternoon wondering if someone kidnapped you and all you have to say for yourself is 'Hi, Mom'?"

"Oh . . . I forgot. We were playing space wars and—"

"I don't care what you were playing," I interrupted. "You know the rules. You're to call me and let me know where you are. You've abused your privileges, and I'm going to have to ground you for a week."

After a brief argument, David accepted his punishment. Later in the week, however, he was invited to go roller skating. When I reminded him that he was grounded another two days, I got the full treatment. Two large hazel eyes peered up at me. It was a look of innocence, apology, sadness, and sincerity all rolled into one. He had been practicing it since he learned how to crawl. It was the one look that he knew pierced his mother to the soul.

"Oh, please let me go, Mom. I've learned my lesson already. I promise I'll remember to call you next time. Honest. But please, you gotta let me go skating."

"No," I said, determined to stand firm this time.

"But, Mom," the gentle plea continued. "All my friends will be there. Look, I'll even do the dishes tonight if you let me go. It isn't even my turn."

I was weakening. My legs and back were cramping from premenstrual tension. My head hurt and I was not looking forward to standing in the kitchen. (Didn't I tell you this kid knew my weaknesses?) I heard myself saying "Well, I don't think . . ."

I'd wavered, and the kid moved in with all the finesse of a foreign diplomat. Within minutes he had me lying on the couch with one pillow propped behind my head and one under my legs. I listened contentedly to the tinkling sound of dishes being washed by someone other than me and relaxed with my warm cup of peppermint tea.

Maybe I shouldn't have given in, but I rationalized that he had been grounded for five days. And, after all, he *had* apologized, and said he'd learned his lesson. Besides . . . he was really a nice boy. And nowhere in the Bible did it say a boy should call his mother when he changed houses. True, he needed to learn obedience, but . . . everyone is entitled to one mistake. So I closed my eyes and decided that next time, I'd be firmer.

There's an inconsistency within most mothers that is both emotional and physical. There are times I can be the perfect disciplinarian. I can handle ten crises in a day and not be thwarted. Other times I *am* the crisis. I've never met anyone who has managed to be continually consistent. Have you?

Aside from the problem of variables in our bodies, there is the problem of differences between spouses. My husband and I agreed completely on what our children needed to learn in order to become productive, responsible adults. We just didn't always see eye-to-eye on the method. I am a softie. I believe in discipline and logical consequences, but unfortunately, I have a lenient streak. My husband, on the other hand, is a sterner disciplinarian.

As long as we discussed our differences and tried to balance each other out, we were fine. But it didn't always happen. There were times when, no matter how hard we tried, we failed.

Finally, what if, in your desire to discipline your child appropriately, you miss the mark? Because of anger, fear, or frustration your punishment is severe. When you've had a chance to think it over, you realize you overreacted. Does pride and a feeling that you must be consistent keep you from going to the child and admitting you were too harsh and have decided to ease up?

Some of us might admit we made a mistake. Some might stand their ground. Who is right . . . who is wrong? It doesn't really matter. The point is, no matter how hard we try, there will be periods of inconsistency for all of us.

So what do we do? Bury ourselves in guilt because we couldn't maintain the consistency set forth by the experts? I did that for a while. But fortunately, I've learned not to make unnecessary guilt trips anymore. I'll be sharing the secrets of escaping the guilt factory in the next chapter, but meanwhile here are a few more observations I've made about discipline.

When weaving a fabric, fixing mistakes is not so difficult, provided you catch the error early on and rework it. If, however, you look back on your work and see a major flaw near the beginning, you will have a long and tedious job correcting the mistake.

When disciplining children and setting boundaries we should make our expectations reasonable. While we certainly want to encourage high standards and teach children to strive for excellence, we don't want to apply the kind of pressure that can lead a child to despair.

The Problem with Perfection

Sometimes Mom and Dad attempt to discipline their children into a state of perfection. This creates large numbers of adults and kids who stagger under the burden of low self-esteem. At the base of their relentless struggles lies a parent who could never be satisfied.

Nancy, a seventeen-year-old, told me, "I feel so stupid. I'm doing the best I can, but I'm never good enough. My mom is always saying, 'That's nice, dear, but . . .' Then she tells me how to do it better. Why can't she ever just be happy with the way I am?"

In a small bedroom that was once her bright young daughter's, a mother sits in silence. She holds a letter now wrinkled and faded from a year's worth of tears. Her daughter had been a brilliant student, class president. But a year ago they'd found her dead, an empty bottle of pills on the nightstand. She'd left a note. "Dear Mom and Dad. I was dropped from Honor Society today. I just couldn't face you. I'm sorry, Kim."

The rocking chair creaks in a gentle rhythm with Mama's soft lament. "If only I had told her the grades didn't matter. If only I'd said, 'I love you for who you are, not for what you do.'"

God does not expect perfection in us any more than we can expect perfection in our children. In her book *What Is a Family?* Edith Schaeffer writes,

When people insist on perfection or nothing, they get nothing.
. . . The waste of what could be, by demanding what cannot
be, is something we all have lived through in certain periods of
our lives, but which we need to put behind us with resolve.[4]

It's a dramatic illustration, I know. And the last thing I
want to do is send you on another guilt trip. It's just that I've
seen what discipline that demands perfection can do. As we
discipline and guide our children onto the right paths, let's
be certain they know beyond a doubt that our love isn't based
on performance.

While disciplining children is a serious business, let's take
care that we don't lose our perspective on the goal, which is
not perfection but self-control, high self-esteem, and obedience to God.

Logical Consequences

One of the best methods for teaching discipline is to allow
for logical consequences. There are logical consequences for
every wrongdoing. We as parents can carry them through or
we can sidestep them. I'd like to illustrate with a short story.

It seems this mother—we'll call her Betty—decided to
clean her son Jason's room the day after Halloween. (He was
a neat kid and she never had to clean his room. However,
this day she decided it needed cleaning.)

Betty finally found Jason's Halloween treats and rummaged
through them "to make sure there was no danger lurking," she
told herself, even though she'd made a thorough inspection the
night before. Several of the caramels peered at her seductively
through their clear cellophane wrappers, but she resisted.

Then she saw them—eight miniature, unwrapped Snick-
ers bars stretched lazily across the windowsill. She felt herself give in to temptation.

"He won't miss just one," Betty said in a muffled voice as she chewed one chocolate, nutty caramel delight.

By the end of the day, she'd eaten them all.

Jason came home from school and promptly blamed his three-year-old brother Sam for eating his candy.

A guilty but valiant Betty stepped in to take the blame. "I ate them, Jase."

Jason's mouth dropped open in surprise. "But, Mom, you're on Weight Watchers."

"I'm really sorry, son. I know I shouldn't have . . . but they were just sitting there begging me to eat them. I couldn't say no."

"Oh, well. That's okay." Jason shrugged his shoulders and turned away. "I wasn't going to eat them anyway. Those are the ones Scooter [their dog] licked."

Logical consequences are for everyone. Don't be afraid to let your children suffer a few. Adults have to.

The Meanest Mother in the World

One of the things you'll find as you involve yourself in the discipline of a child is that you'll undoubtedly be referred to as a "mean mother."

This delightful letter appeared several years ago in an Ann Landers column:

I had the meanest mother in the world. While other kids had candy for breakfast, I had to eat cereal, eggs and toast. While other kids had Cokes and candy for lunch, I had a sandwich. As you can guess, my dinner was different from other kids' dinners too.

My mother insisted on knowing where we were at all times. You'd think we were on a chain gang or something. She had to know who our friends were and what we were doing.

I am ashamed to admit it, but she actually had the nerve to break the child labor law. She made us work. We had to wash dishes, make the beds and learn how to cook.

That woman must have stayed awake nights thinking up things for us kids to do. And she always insisted that we tell the truth, the whole truth and nothing but the truth.

By the time we were teenagers, our life became even more unbearable. None of this tooting the car horn for us to come running; she embarrassed us to no end by insisting that the boys come to the door to get us.

I forgot to mention that most of our friends were allowed to date at the mature ages of twelve and thirteen, but our old-fashioned mother refused to let us date until we were fifteen. She really raised a bunch of squares. None of us was ever arrested for shoplifting or busted for dope. And who do we have to thank for this? You're right, our mean mother.

I'm trying to raise my children to stand a little straighter and taller, and I am secretly tickled to pieces when my children call me mean. I thank God for giving me the meanest mother in the world. Our country doesn't need a good five-cent cigar. It needs more mean mothers like mine.

While being a mean mother won't necessarily guarantee that our kids will never get into trouble, it is a safeguard we would do well to incorporate into our mothering.

It does warm a mother's heart when her children rise up and call her mean.

Discipline is often a difficult task. What happens when the cookie jar is empty and no one confesses? Who gets disciplined? It's time for a little detective work, and who's better qualified than a mom? She has the ultimate weapon for solving mysteries—intuition.

A Mother Knows

As an author, I sometimes find I've written a word, phrase, or idea that just doesn't seem right. I get a vague feeling something is wrong. I can stop and fix that part of my manuscript immediately or leave it alone and hope it was just my mind playing tricks on me. Invariably, however, if I don't take care of it, the editor or one of my readers will point out the problem.

What I encounter in my writing goes for kids, too. Use your intuition when it comes to rearing your children.

Marge, a friend from out of state, told me this story: "My daughter, Tracy, brought home a friend one day. I knew the minute I met this kid there'd be trouble. But I didn't want to embarrass my daughter or her friend. After all, what if I was wrong? The girl, Cindy, was perfectly behaved, polite, and I finally decided I'd made a mistake in my first impression.

"I hadn't," Marge went on to say. "Cindy and Tracy were picked up for shoplifting a week later. Tracy was in tears. She told me she'd had a feeling about Cindy but shrugged it aside because the girl was fun to be around. Some fun!"

Marge and her daughter both learned to use their intuition.

When you get that nagging feeling that something is wrong, act on it. Otherwise, you'll get caught and have to go back and fix the damage. Of course, when it comes to your children's friends and what your kids do away from home, you may not be able to interfere. But you can sniff out trouble and raise the warning flag. Sometimes when you talk to your children about your concerns, they will be able to make the right decision on their own. Other times, they may have to learn from experience.

My kids have been shocked to find out just how much Mom knew about what mischief they'd been up to. Mothers seem to have a built-in radar to help them:

- know that little Randy is sticking his hand in the cookie jar when he should be in his room taking a nap.
- know it wasn't the kid down the street who broke Dad's favorite chair.
- know the ten dollars in her billfold didn't just *disappear*.
- know when Julie is lying about what she was doing out until 1:00 A.M.
- know when danger is imminent.

A kid needs a mom who acknowledges and uses her intuition.

A Flaw in the Masterpiece

As we work to weave in discipline, there is one aspect we must deal with—uncertainty. No matter how careful we are, flaws will creep into the weaving. We will look back and see open, vulnerable areas. Teachers, peers, television, and others come in and out of the child's life, adding threads we might not have chosen. Even we at times weave in inappropriate or discolored strings. We may look back to find a flaw that has caused a weakness in character.

Mothering is an awesome responsibility. I am so grateful I have a God who understands that I cannot in my own strength create a perfectly woven masterpiece. I'm thankful He can mend the torn and frayed edges. I'm also glad He said things like, "My grace is sufficient for thee: for my strength is made perfect in weakness . . ." (2 Cor. 12:9 KJV).

As mothers, most of us do the best we can in weaving threads of discipline into our children. But there is a certain gamble. In rearing children, even if we feel we've done everything right, there is no guarantee that someone won't come along and undo the threads we've woven. Or, we may look back and feel we did nearly everything wrong, but somehow our kids made it through. Sometimes we lose. Sometimes we win.

The secret to weaving in the threads of discipline lies in doing the best we can and trusting God to fill in the gaps.

9

An Unexpected Tour of the Guilt Factory

As we close the door on discipline and move on down the corridor, how many of you feel as if you're dragging along a ball and chain with *Guilt* written all over it? Are you feeling tired and maybe a bit discouraged? There's a lot to being the kind of mom kids need. You'd think they'd pay more for the job.

Maybe it's time, in our tour of the mansion, to take a brief rest. Here at the end of the hall is an easy chair. Let's sit a minute.

We no sooner get seated when the room begins to move. No, it's not the room. It's us. The panel behind us and the portion of the floor holding the chair are turning. In a matter of seconds the lovely hallway has disappeared and before us is a damp, dungeonlike room. Cobwebs from centuries of dust hang heavy from every corner. Musty smells of rotten wood and moss-covered stone fill our senses. We can hear the splash of water and a low, unearthly growl.

As our eyes adjust to the dim light of a candle, we can barely make out shapes of—no, it can't be. It looks like an ancient torture chamber—a stretching rack, a ball and chain, a guillotine, and (gulp) even an alligator pit.

Built-in Guilt

This is part of being a mother? Maybe you're wondering where our explorations have led us. This, my friends and fellow mothers, is the famous guilt factory.

I decided to stop for a quick tour, because every mother's heart comes equipped with a room like this. And every mother ends up taking a trip through it at some time or other. Sometimes we come out unblemished, but more often than not, we end up wearing the ball and chain on a permanent basis.

At one time I was a frequent visitor to the guilt factory. I would often let guilt stretch me out on the rack until I literally ached. Other times I'd lay my head across the sharp blade of the guillotine and wait for the lever to be pulled. Fortunately, no one ever pulled it. Most of the time, though, I settled for the ball and chain.

I had been led to believe that ultimately I was responsible for my children's behavior and when they messed up, it was a direct reflection on me. I blamed myself not only for the things I really had done wrong but also for those things over which I had no control.

When my children hit the explosive teen years and made some wrong choices, I visited this room on a regular basis. Unfortunately, there were quite a few people who were more than willing to open the door for me.

In my book *Have You Hugged Your Teenager Today?* I dedicated three chapters to helping parents get out of the guilt factory and lock the door behind them. I'll cover a few of those basics now.

Standing Trial

First of all, I'd like you to think about why you feel guilty. If you're visiting the guilt factory on a regular basis, perhaps it's because you really are doing something wrong.

For example, Alice, a mother of two boys under five, suffers from frequent pangs of guilt. Every morning she hustles around trying to get herself ready for work. She seldom has a chance to give the kids a bath and is lucky to even get their night diapers changed before she packs them up, straps them in the car, and runs them to the sitter.

"Sorry," she says in a limp apology. "I didn't have time to feed them . . . and . . . Andy is soaked."

Alice leaves them clinging to the sitter, whiny, runny noses, and wet diapers, relieved to have someone else cope with the mess. She goes to her job and puts in a full day's work. When she picks up her children they cry, because they'd rather stay with the sitter. By the time she gets the kids home and supper on the table, she's spent.

Alice rushes through the bedtime routine with the children. She decides to skip their baths tonight. After she puts them to bed, she can hear them crying in the other room. Guilt washes over her, and she remembers hearing somewhere that you can spoil a kid by rocking him to sleep. She doesn't dare start, they'd want it every night, and she couldn't. . . . Guilt nudges her, but she shoves it aside and turns on her favorite television comedy for a few laughs.

She'll be glad when morning comes and she can drop off the kids again. At least at work, she's appreciated.

Alice *should* be feeling guilty, because she is neglecting her children. In order for the guilt feeling to go away, Alice must face it. She needs to examine the priorities in her life and place her children in higher esteem.

God uses true guilt to show us we're heading the wrong way. When we do examine our guilty feelings and realize we've done wrong, there is only one solution: We must repent—meaning we apologize to God and to our children and stop doing the wrong. God then promises us release from that guilt.

Guilty until Proven Innocent

There is another kind of guilt, however, that throws us into the dungeon. After we have examined our actions and realize we are not at fault, it still happens. It is a kind of guilt that hounds us—even after we have been released by God. It's called false guilt.

One good friend, Marty, had been suffering from every torture in the guilt factory. Her daughter Candi ran away from home at fourteen and got pregnant. Marty had worked outside the home since Candi was seven. Candi's father had died in an accident.

Marty and Candi had a good relationship. Marty tried to teach her daughter all the right things. She never taught her how to steal or to try drugs. In fact, Marty taught her the dangers of that kind of life.

But Candi found some friends who taught her everything they knew. When Candi left home, Marty blamed herself. She went into the guilt factory with the blessing of her friends and family. Friends insinuated that if she hadn't had to work, it wouldn't have happened. She was labeled guilty until proven innocent, judged and hung without a trial.

Marty had fallen into the trap of false guilt. Fortunately, Marty is learning that she shouldn't keep what doesn't belong to her and is gradually leaving guilt in the dungeon where it belongs.

I understand how Marty felt. I've taken my turn in the guilt factory numerous times. I might still be there if my daughter hadn't given me some wise advice.

"It Wasn't Your Fault, Mom"

Caryl had always been an easy child to raise. As I recall, she got a total of two spankings throughout her entire childhood. She seemed to be a nearly ideal child—a good student, obedient—what more could a parent ask for?

In her sixteenth year, we saw some subtle changes, but then, why wouldn't we? She was turning from a child to a woman, and some mood swings were inevitable. She had gone through some major changes in her life as well. Injuries knocked her out of competition in gymnastics, and she was forced to find new interests and friends.

We thought she'd handled it well. She hadn't.

My husband and I had gone on a business trip, leaving Caryl to stay with her grandmother during our absence. When we arrived home a month later, our daughter had changed.

She greeted us at the door with a wide smile and warm hugs. "There's something I have to tell you, Mom," she said. "Last weekend I became a Christian."

My mouth fell open. "But you've always been a Christian."

"No. Not really. I went to Sunday school and church, but it was just because you made me. It never meant anything to me before."

"But how—what happened?" I stammered.

"Well, that's the hard part. For the last year, I've been pretty mixed up. You know all the times I stayed at Jan's house?"

"Yes."

"Well, we usually didn't stay there. We'd go out to parties. Her folks would lie to you and tell you we were outside 'cause they thought you were being too strict."

"I can't believe this."

"Mom, I couldn't even ask you to let me go to those parties. I knew you wouldn't let me."

"Were you drinking?"

She nodded. "I'm not proud of what I did, Mom. In fact, last week we got in trouble with the police. I was so scared you'd find out. I didn't want you to be disappointed in me. I decided to kill myself. I didn't think I could face you and Dad again."

My knuckles turned white as I clasped my hands together. The shock of what I was hearing blocked any meaningful words from making their way out of my mouth. *Suicide? I cried inside. How could this have happened? What kind of mother am I? I should have never gone on that trip.*

"I was trying to get the gun together when the phone rang," she continued. "It was a guy I'd never met, but he'd seen my name on his church roster [we'd visited the church a few times] and recognized it. His brother was in Youth With a Mission with David. Anyway, he asked me to come to a youth retreat that weekend. I don't know why—I really didn't want to—but I said yes. I went, and a lady, one of the counselors, started talking to me. Before I knew it, I was telling her everything. She said the Lord still loved me, and I could be forgiven for all the stuff I'd done—even lying to you."

"Of course, honey. We've talked about forgiveness."

"I know, Mom, but it just didn't sink in. Anyway, she told me about how Jesus died for me, and that all I had to do was ask forgiveness and I would be saved. Well, I did, and I committed myself to Jesus. Now I need you and Dad to forgive me. I know I'll need to be punished. . . ."

I didn't know whether to be happy or angry. I pulled her into my arms and cried. "Of course I'll forgive you. But I don't understand how you could have—oh, I feel so terrible." I drew back from the circle of her arms to look at her. "I should have known something was wrong."

"No, Mom, you couldn't have known what was going on. I didn't want you to."

"But . . . oh, baby, we came so close to losing you. What did I do wrong? What could I have done differently so this wouldn't have happened?"

For a moment I felt like a child, while my daughter spoke to me with all the wisdom of a mom. "Don't blame yourself.

You've been a great mother. You taught me right from wrong. What happened was my fault. I knew it wasn't right. I think maybe I had to go through this, to make my own decisions. I had to come to God in my own way. Because of what happened, I have a very strong testimony to share with other teenagers."

In telling this story I don't want you to think for one moment it was as easy as it might appear on paper. It would take a whole book to describe the pain our family went through. My point is that Caryl, not her mother, had made some wrong choices.

I hadn't been the perfect mom, but I'd done my best. I'd woven strength into Caryl's fabric. She had been pulled and stretched in many ways. She weakened some, even tore a little. God mended her worn places and stitched up the tears. She made some errors, but in the end, she chose God's way.

When we do wrong as mothers, guilt can be dealt with swiftly and surely by accepting the blame and saying, "I'm sorry." Then God can get on with the business of forgiving. That way, we spend very little time in the guilt factory.

Kids need moms who spend less time feeling guilty and more time loving, hugging, kissing, laughing, and getting the job of mothering done.

Now, let's get out of this hole in the ground. I don't know about you, but I need some fresh air.

10

The Playroom

Guilt is a terrible place to be. The worst of it is that you don't need a key to get into the guilt factory—it has the key to get into you.

After our trip through guilt, what we need now is a lighter look at motherhood. Ready for the next door?

Go ahead and open it. Sitting in the center of the floor are three small children. Their laughter rises on the air as if hitching a ride on the hundreds of rainbow bubbles escaping from the children's bubble pipes.

Colorful balloon bouquets wave in the gentle stir of the air as they wait to be bounced, bopped, and popped. Three porcelain-faced clown dolls smile beneath their fake frowns. Teddy bears and toy soldiers peek from an open toy chest in the corner.

Rain slashes against the window, the sky hovers in shades of gray. Outside there is a storm, yet in this room lies a treasure more valuable than a golden sun—happiness, laughter, and fun.

Kids need a mom who will teach them to laugh. A joyful heart can overcome nearly all obstacles.

The Key to a Happy Heart

Few people in this world have ever found the key to happiness. It is such a simple thing really. We receive hints from people who encourage us to "stop and smell the roses." Sometimes in fleeting moments we think we have found it, only to have the joy squashed out of us by the crushing realities of life.

Many try to uncover happiness by surrounding themselves with treasures such as newer cars, bigger houses, furs, and jewelry, or by changing the people around them. "If only I had a maid . . . if only I had an obedient child . . . if only I had a job . . . if only I could stay home and raise my kids instead of working . . . then I would be happy."

The key is a simple one. It's given to everyone. Your happiness depends on whether you decide to use the key to unlock a treasure house of joy or leave it hidden under the mat.

What is the key? Simply this:

When life hands you lemons . . . make lemonade.

Too simple? Then perhaps you will want to read about growing positive attitudes in yourself and your kids in chapter 12. But for now, let's hear it for laughter.

Loving Enough to Laugh

In Proverbs, wise King Solomon tells us, "A cheerful heart is good medicine, but a downcast spirit dries up the bones" (Prov. 17:22 RSV). Did you know there is medical evidence to prove that theory?

Research suggests that laughter releases morphinelike substances called endorphins in the brain that cause pleasure and relieve pain. Many in the medical profession now recognize laughter as a very real medicine—a mood elevator and an analgesic.

Laughter is also a boon to physical fitness. A hearty belly laugh will match jogging time for time. In other words, twenty minutes laughing and twenty minutes jogging can have the same physical benefit.

My children learned how to laugh. My husband used to tell the children that if they grew any taller their feet wouldn't touch the ground and other tall tales. We'd make up crazy puns and tell jokes.

Laughter is a natural spring that bubbles up inside us. Having been created in the image of God, we are born with the ability to laugh. But often it is stifled at an early age, when we show children displeasure at their giggling. Can you remember the last time you laughed so hard you cried, fell to the floor, and rolled from side to side, holding your aching tummy? If you can't, it's been too long.

There's only one catch to teaching the art of joyfulness to your children: You have to know how to have fun.

Having Fun

When was the last time you had fun? So often we adults fall into the role of proper, straitlaced, dignified, boring grown-ups. Somewhere on the path to growing up we lose our childlike wonder. We become goal oriented and focused on the routine and mundane. We may focus so hard on rearing our children, we forget to enjoy them.

I think if I could do one thing over again as a mom, it might be to commit myself to having even more fun. I often took life too seriously. I sometimes wish I'd used my water pistol with a little more regularity. I might take life less seriously and be a little more like my son-in-law who rarely misses an opportunity to *play.*

My daughter and her husband, Ben, recently moved to California, and my husband and I had gone for a visit this past May—and yes, we were there on Mother's Day. For my Mother's Day gift they took me to Knott's Berry Farm. What a blast. While I couldn't stomach some of the wilder roller-coaster rides, I had a great time watching my husband and Ben, the grown-up kids, as they screamed through the park.

They went on practically everything, and I think they had more fun than my four grandchildren. I thoroughly enjoyed being a kid for the day myself just hanging out, talking, and walking with my daughter and grandchildren, watching the seal and dolphin shows, dropping out of the sky in a parachute ride, and shooting the rapids. They gave me a precious gift that day. They gave me fun.

When was the last time you gave up your adultness and let yourself slip into the hilarious, carefree role of a child? We have inside ourselves a parent and a child. I don't think God ever intended that as we grow into adulthood, we forsake the child. Didn't He say, "Let the children come to me, and do not hinder them; for to such belongs the kingdom of heaven" (Matt. 19:14 RSV)? "Truly, I say to you, whoever does not receive the kingdom of God like a child shall not enter it" (Mark 10:15 RSV).

For the sake of having fun, be frivolous for a change. It won't mar your image. Go for a wild run on the beach with your hair flying in every direction. Create a sand castle. Write "I love you" in the sand. Fly a kite and let the wind take your soul along for the ride. Make a mud pie. Let a puppy lick your face. Climb a mountain. Drink your fill from an icy stream. Make a snow angel or a snowman.

If you're still having trouble with your laugh life, try a little game playing. We occasionally indulge in the "What If" game. You take an ordinary person, place, or thing and let your imagination fly.

For example: The other day my husband and I were walking on the beach. I commented about how fast the sandpipers (actually plovers) scurry along the beach.

"Yeah," my husband said, "they're cute now, but what if they were twenty feet tall?"

"And what if they ran twenty times faster than they do now?"

Can you imagine a herd of twenty-foot-tall sandpipers zipping along the beach at a hundred miles an hour? Those plovers would pulverize every human on the beach.

Yes, the "What If" game can get ridiculous, but it's a sure way to get you laughing.

Recently I saw a bumper sticker on a little 4x4 truck. It read, "The one with the most toys when he dies, wins." How sad. Chances are he'll have more toys than anyone could ever use, but is he really having fun? Real fun doesn't cost money—it just takes a little time.

The people who have taught me the most about play are the children. If I forget, I simply think about them. I especially remember a precious moment with my granddaughter Corisa. She was four at the time. We'd gone to the park to play, and I gave her a push on the swing. I couldn't help noticing the look of sheer delight on her face. Wondering what was going on in her head, I asked, "What's swinging like?"

She tipped her head back and thought for a moment, then replied, "Nanna, it's like a summer day." I often think about her comment and try to capture the awe and magic of the world around me, delighting in life as she did for at least a few minutes out of every day.

Just as there is time for being an adult, for being wise and grown-up in one's thinking, there is time to be a child. My poem expresses this thought.

> Become like a child again?
> Capture cloud creatures,
> touch the breeze,
> and bend rainbows?
> Play hide-and-seek in giant oaks
> and splash in rainy day puddles?
> Absurd!

Or is it?
Perhaps we could regain
innocence . . .
faith . . .
trust.
Trust ourselves . . .
Our world . . .
To God's grown-up hands.

A kid needs a mom who still knows how to be a kid and have fun.

11

The Library

The next room along the mansion's hallway houses perhaps the greatest wealth in the world. The riches lining the walls here "introduce us to people and places we wouldn't ordinarily know." They are "a gateway into a broader world of wonder, of beauty, of delight and adventure. . . ." They bring us "experiences that make us grow, that add something to our inner stature. . . ."[1]

A desk, a pencil, a notebook, and mahogany shelves filled with books wait for someone. Your child? On the desk is a piece of blank paper. The paper is a symbol of a child's mind, waiting to be filled. ". . . a young child, a fresh, uncluttered mind, a world before him—to what treasure will you lead him? With what will you furnish his spirit?"[2]

There were so many things I wanted to teach my children, yet before and while I taught them, I had to learn. I had to learn their interests and talents, their temperaments and uniqueness.

Know Your Child

If you doubt the importance of knowing your kids, here's a story that may help you understand what teaching a child without knowing him can do.

Tommy hurried to his seat in the morning kindergarten class. He clutched his school box, for in it lay his favorite of all toys: crayons and paper. Tommy loved to draw. He could draw birds, houses, trees, and even people.

His teacher smiled. "Take out your crayons and paper. Today we're going to draw flowers."

Oh, good, thought Tommy. *I love to draw flowers.* Tommy reached for a red crayon and began to draw a rose.

"Tommy." The teacher stood beside his desk. "Not that way. Turn over your paper and draw the way I show you on the board."

So Tommy picked up the pink crayon, as the teacher said, and drew a flower, just as the teacher did.

A year later, Tommy hurries into another school in another town.

Today his new teacher smiles and says, "Class, today we're going to draw. Take out your crayons and paper."

Tommy does as the teacher says. He doesn't like to draw much anymore. He sits and waits for the teacher to continue.

The teacher stops at his desk. "Tommy." She kneels down beside him. "Is something the matter? Why haven't you started your drawing?"

"I can't draw it by myself. I'm waiting for you to show me how."

Tommy's first teacher kept her class in order. She taught her students to mimic her instead of allowing them to develop their individual talents. As a result, Tommy lost his fresh, creative freedom. Will he ever get it back? Will he be the one, when older, to say, "I never could draw a straight line"?

What a tragedy when children are pushed and shoved, however well meant, into a shape that is a parent's or teacher's instead of being allowed to grow into the shape that is theirs alone.

Take a few minutes—right now if you want. I can wait. Find out:

- What is your child's favorite color . . . toy . . . book . . . song?
- What would your child most like to do on a rainy day?
- What is your child's best friend's name? Who are the friend's parents? What are the friend's hobbies?
- What does your child want to be when he or she grows up?

Those are just a few questions to help you get started. Find out as much as you can about your children. Know them and the unique personalities that go into making them the special children who have been entrusted into your care.

Creative Mothering

Besides coming to know my children, one of the challenges of being a mother was trying to offer a full supply of "things to do when there was nothing to do" and at the same time provide tools for learning.

Kids today live in a fast-paced society. In order to compete with all the world has to offer, we'll need to use our imaginations to come up with interesting, exciting options.

What all of us mothers love to hear (and always during the busiest part of the day) is, "Mom, what's there to do? I'm bored."

One mother I know developed a "things to do" jar. This is an extension of the famous job jar created to entice husbands off the couch and into the fix-it realm.

You might want to develop two jars—one for projects requiring little or no supervision on Mom's part, and another requiring family participation. The jars may contain hundreds of creative ideas such as:

- Make a papier-mâché zoo. (When my children were smaller, we would make papier-mâché masks. By using

117

a large balloon as a base, I helped them create their costumes. One year we made a pink bunny head and a Winnie-the-Pooh. For Pooh, we covered the head with honey-
colored fur and made a fur jumpsuit to complete the
outfit. Pooh survived both kids and got passed along to
a neighbor.)

- Take a hike. (This is a great time for nature study and
  in-depth conversations.)
- Make clay woven baskets. (Modeling clay or Play-Doh
  is a great outlet. I still vent my hostilities and calm my
  inner savage beast by getting my hands into clay.)
- Color in your new coloring book. (Along with books,
  you may want to have a supply of new craft items for
  an occasional lift.)
- Jump in a lake. (Go swimming.)
- Draw a mural on the wall. (Since most kids find the
  empty space of a wall an irresistible canvas for their masterpiece, why not consider a large washable panel as part
  of your decor? Strategically placed in a living or family
  room, it can serve as a conversation piece when friends
  drop by, and what a boost to the kid's ego to have his or
  her picture displayed in such a prominent place.)
- Read a book. (Give them a choice of titles or, better yet,
  read to them.)

Read to Your Children

Make it a point to read to your children every day. This
serves several purposes. It assures that you spend time with
them each day. It gives them a love and respect for books.
Reading teaches and helps children develop a desire to learn
more. Through books children can enter into exciting adven-
tures and at the same time learn important principles. One

of my favorite children's books is *Bombus the Bumblebee* by Elsie Larson (see the suggested reading list). It's a wonderful book for building and restoring self-esteem.

My children always loved reading, and I know it was because I read to them. Now, as a grandmother, I write stories as well. I write a series, the Jennie McGrady Mysteries, for children as young as ten and as old as eighty-two. One of my greatest joys is discovering that a teacher or parent has been reading the series to their kids. Teachers and parents often use mysteries and adventure books in the classrooms and at home to stimulate and encourage kids to read and also as a springboard to discuss various topics the books might deal with. Mine, for example, deal with issues and problems children face every day in our society: environment, boy-girl relationships, broken homes, guns and kids, and prejudice, to name a few.

Having a history as a pediatric nurse and counselor, I care very much about children. In writing my books, I want to give them a good story, but I also want them to develop the ability to cope with their own situations and to learn to solve problems. I want to empower them with survival skills and teach them the clear difference between right and wrong.

Their own feelings are validated through the characters they read about. Kids tell me my characters are very real. They laugh, they hurt, they cry, they become angry. They don't always get along with their parents. They are not perfect, which endears them to kids of all ages. Like many authors of children's books, I have set certain standards and will not use gratuitous sex, violence, or obscene language. I firmly believe in the old adage "garbage in—garbage out."

Kids are enchanted by stories. Why not take advantage of their love of adventure and put books in their hands that will also have redeeming value?

Not all authors pay attention to how their writing affects children, so you'll want to be careful in your book selections and be certain they meet the criteria you have set for your children. I recently purchased a book for my nephew and ended up not giving it to him because the main character (the hero) had casually stolen a bike and suffered no consequences for his actions.

Some pulp fiction for kids exists simply as hype to earn the author and publisher a lot of money. At an author reception in New York editors of kids' mysteries were asked to tell about their publishing houses and what types of books they produced. My editor said she wanted books with integrity: "We want books that will uplift, encourage, and entertain kids as well as adults."

After she spoke, the editor for a publishing house that develops a popular horror book series said, "Our books have absolutely no redeeming value." He laughed and added, "But they make us a lot of money."

Sadly, many children are for the most part nonreaders. I'd like to change that, and if you are an avid reader, chances are you would too. Rather than invest in video games or software, I buy my nephews, nieces, and grandchildren books. I want to continue the reading tradition, not only because I write but because of the enjoyment and education reading can bring.

I recently saw an ad in a newspaper picturing a guy sitting on top of a mountain of broken-down computer parts. One might think he'd be depressed, or downtrodden, but on his face was a look of pure pleasure. Why? He had rediscovered books. Books are low-cost, low-maintenance gifts that require no batteries or electrical outlets.

All kids need to operate books is an imagination and the ability to read. And, of course, moms and dads who will steer them in the right direction.

Today, to promote literacy among the younger generation, I encourage hundreds of children to read and write by doing book talks and teaching classes on developing intriguing characters and plots. Many authors are willing to visit schools and libraries to promote literacy and to encourage children in the art of reading and writing.

Build a Library of Good Books

If you enjoy reading to your children, you'll want to have a variety of books on hand. My children developed their own libraries early on and still place great value on their collections of classics. In fact, those same books are being passed down to their children.

You'll find the titles of several books that keep giving— even when the covers are closed—in the suggested reading list at the back of this book.

Being a creative mother takes time, but it will be worth the effort when, as your children get older, you hear them reminisce with smiles in their voices:

"We used to . . ."

"I'll never forget . . ."

"Remember when . . ."

"That was the best time I ever had."

You will not be the only one who teaches your child. Yet, it is your responsibility to monitor what material he or she learns. While we can't control everything that goes into our children's minds, we can have some input.

If you enroll your child in day care or preschool, public, or even private schools, you'll want to check out the teachers and the curriculum. The more hours your child spends in an institution, the more important your input. You may even decide to keep your child out of learning institutions completely.

Who Will Educate Your Child?

Proverbs 22:6 KJV tells us, "Train up a child in the way he should go: and when he is old, he will not depart from it."

They are wise words and could be comforting ones—if we were indeed training our children. Unfortunately, most of the training of children these days is not done by parents. It is done by schools, television, and peers.

Exposing our children to experiences outside the family and home can be beneficial, as long as we oversee the experience. But too often our children are taught the opposite of what we believe in situations where parents are losing control.

Many parents today have sought and found a solution to this dilemma by educating their children at home or in a setting in which they maintain a greater control over what the child learns.

Home schooling is becoming more and more popular as concern over public schools grows. The articles on home schooling are impressive. I'll admit I was skeptical at first. I remember sending my kids off to school with a huge sigh of relief. Alone . . . I had time alone. I didn't know about home schooling then, and I might have rejected it at first as an ugly demon trying to devour my few hours of peace.

Home schooling may not be the time-consuming thing many parents fear. Parents do not have to incorporate four to six hours of teaching a day into their already overloaded lives. In fact Dr. Raymond Moore, Ed.D., developmental psychologist and founder of the Hewitt Foundation, said this: "If a mother or father formally instructs sixty to ninety minutes daily and spends a like period supervising study, the average child will excel classroom children."[3]

I have spoken with many parents who have chosen to educate their children at home. The results have been very positive. One woman said, "At first I thought I would go crazy, but once the children were away from the disruptive influence of the classroom and we established a routine, their behavior improved and so did their concentration and ability to learn."

One of the primary problems I see in the public schools is a lack of moral integrity. As one teacher told me, "Teachers are not allowed to teach religion or morality because they can't risk offending anyone." In addition, the academic standard has declined seriously over the years and students in public schools in the United States score consistently low.

We often hear about the lack of safety in schools due to weapons and drug use. In many schools children are having to pass through metal detectors as they enter the doors of the building.

I could go on to list more problems, but you probably have a list of your own.

Margaret Mead once said, "My grandmother wanted me to get an education so she kept me out of school." An interesting theory and one with which many parents today fully agree.

Some of you may choose to send your children to a private school; some may choose home schooling. Many of you, however, may not have the time or funding for either and must utilize the public school system. However your children receive their formal education, you will want to oversee their curriculum. Keep in close contact with your child's teacher. If by chance you are unhappy with that teacher, ask that your child be transferred. While there are some poor teachers, there are also many excellent, dedicated teachers who share your value system. Research the schools in your area. Even if your children go to a public school, you are ultimately responsible for their education. As a taxpayer, you have a say about how the public schools in your area are run. Why not exercise that right?

Garbage In—Garbage Out

In an earlier segment I mentioned the term "garbage in—garbage out." This is a term often used by computer people. It simply means your computer will only be as good as the components and software you put in it. In a real sense, this principle applies to human minds. For people, though, there is also the element of subliminal suggestion. Advertisers use this method to urge us to buy their products. How many of you get thirsty or hungry watching advertisements for colas and hamburgers? Here's a story to illustrate my point.

Ann's son, Chris, went to the library and checked out *Willie Wonka and the Chocolate Factory* by Roald Dahl. He read for a while every day. And every day he'd beg for a candy bar. The more time he spent reading his book about sweets, the more he craved sweets.

Ann realized that her son was being influenced by the power of suggestion. We can apply the same principle to other types of books or videos, television or movies that might be more harmful. If we allow a child to dwell on violence in books or on-screen, there is a good chance he or she will begin to crave more. Tragically, a craving for guns and explosives turned a fifteen-year-old student from Springfield, Oregon, into a cold-blooded murderer. He gunned down his parents, then went to his school and opened fire in a cafeteria, killing two students and injuring twenty-five. Perhaps the greatest shock is that this type of violent activity is on the increase.

Eventually what is fed into our minds on a regular basis comes out in actions.

Ann stressed to her son the importance of filling his mind with information that would produce worthwhile and acceptable actions. It may not be a bad idea to print the words, "GARBAGE IN—GARBAGE OUT" on a large poster paper and affix it to a conspicuous place in your child's room or study area.

Carefully consider what is going into your child's brain. Weed out as much of the harmful influence as possible. Perhaps it is nothing. Perhaps I am an alarmist, but I can't help but wonder if those seemingly harmless video games with cartoon characters chasing each other, throwing barrels and bombs at bad guys might not be fertile ground for real guns and bombs and violence in the future.

Show-and-Tell

As our children are growing up there are many principles we want to teach them. Concepts are often difficult to teach since a child's attention span is short and they'd rather be having fun than listening to words. Sometimes we need to use a method employed by educators called show-and-tell. First *show* the child with the use of a story or, better yet, a real-life illustration, then *tell* him or her. Let me illustrate.

Say you wanted to teach your child the valuable lesson of unselfishness. You could just tell him or her to share or try to explain the concept of putting others first, but would he or she understand?

Or, you could tell him a story like this, which was handed down by Wilma, a white-haired grandmother and very experienced mother.

How exciting! A mother bird had laid two tiny eggs in a nest almost hidden among the leaves of the tall rosebush that shaded my parents' bedroom window. As a small girl I watched with interest as the days passed. Finally, I saw two wide-open mouths begging for food when their mother was startled into flight.

Almost every day I stopped by the nest after school to visit my new little feathered friends. But one day, to my horror, the sprinkler was trained directly on the rosebush. "Daddy, Daddy!" I cried. "Please turn off the water . . . the birds."

My dad turned off the water and we went to check the bird family. The father bird fluttered frantically from branch to branch in a nearby tree. The mother sat on the nest, her tiny head drooping, her feathers soaked.

I gently lifted her lifeless body from the nest. As I did, two hungry babes opened their mouths for food. It was the ultimate act of unselfishness. That the mother bird had given her life to protect her babies. It reminds me of how Jesus gave His life for me on Calvary.

We couldn't save the baby birds, so I placed them with their mother in a softly lined matchbox and gave them a proper burial. A small wooden cross marked the site in Mama's garden.

You see how much a story can add to your teaching? Watch for happenings in and around your home that illustrate the principles you want to teach your child.

There are hundreds, maybe even thousands, of concepts I wanted my children to learn, but few are as important as these next two. The first is how to handle the inequities life hands us.

Justice Smushtice

In rearing our children, we moms usually try to be fair. However, mothers will be wise not to take the children's idea of fairness too seriously.

I'm not going to try to balance the scales of justice here—on the contrary. I want to point out the injustices.

Life isn't fair. It never has been and it never will be. We are all dished out problems in different portions. In fact, life can be downright hard. And the sooner we learn that fact the better we'll be able to handle life and grow beyond our problems.

I made the mistake of trying to be fair with my kids. Always giving equal amounts of dessert. If I took one to the zoo, I made it a point to take the other one. If I bought a sweater for one, I'd have to buy something of equal value for the other. It eventually became a frustrating battle, because no matter how fair I tried to be, I would often hear those endearing words: "Mom, that's not fair—Caryl got more cake than me."

I suppose to minimize sibling rivalry, a mother must try to be fair to some extent, but . . . there is a limit. And whether we like it or not, something always comes along to tip the scales.

For instance, one child may receive infinitely more scolding than another, simply because he or she insists on learning the hard way or acting out to gain more of your attention. Would it be fair to punish the other child? Of course not.

Rewards and punishments can be directly related to our behavior, but then again, they may not be. Suppose eleven-year-old Cassandra spends an hour a day trying to learn her math skills. Joshua, on the other hand, breezes through a fifteen-minute session and seems bored. On a test at the end of the week, Joshua makes an A while Cassandra drags in with a D. Is that fair?

Is it fair that Randy scores more baskets than Ken? They're both the same height and age. Why can't things be equal?

Who knows? The one thing I do know is that if we keep playing the "life isn't fair" game, we'll just end up miserable. If life keeps tossing you foul balls, there's not much more you can do but to keep swinging. One of these days you'll connect.

Children who learn early to handle and solve problems will be much stronger and capable of surviving in this "unfair" world, than those who were allowed to believe they should receive their fair share.

As I said, life is full of problems. We can teach our children to handle those problems in two different ways. Either we show them how to moan and groan about problems while they multiply, or we teach them the art of problem solving.

The Problem with Earl

In his book *The Road Less Traveled,* M. Scott Peck writes, "Once we truly know that life is difficult—once we truly understand and accept it—then life is no longer difficult. Because once it is accepted, the fact that life is difficult no longer matters."[4]

One day several years ago, my children came running into the house with a problem. It seems a baby squirrel (herein referred to as Earl) had fallen out of his nest, which was located in the upper regions of our tallest fir tree.

What could we do? The first step in problem solving is to accept the fact that you have a problem. Now, I could have turned my back on Earl, but that would have given me bigger problems: (1) how to explain my apathy to the kids; (2) how and where to bury a dead squirrel; and (3) how to deal with guilt.

So, I faced the problem head-on. Now for step two—what could we do with this ball of fuzz with a tail? This step meant brainstorming for possible solutions.

"We could put it back in the nest," David, then ten, advised.

"It's too high," I said.

"I can climb it." He raced away and began to shinny up the rough bark.

"Get down from there!" I yelled.

"I can do it."

"All right," I warned. "But if you fall and break your leg, don't come running to me."

"Why can't we keep him?" Caryl stroked Earl's quivering head.

"Because he's wild, and he'd be happier with his mommy," I said. Then I remembered reading that many animals reject their young if the human scent is on them. "Besides, I don't know what baby squirrels eat."

"How about milk?" injected David, who had given up on his climb.

We brought a small bowl of warm milk and set it in front of Earl. Earl's tiny body shook like Jell-O in an earthquake, but he didn't drink. I put his mouth into the warm liquid. His pink tongue darted out to lick the milk off his chin.

"Maybe he could drink from my doll's baby bottle," Caryl suggested. We tried, but the nipple was too big.

"I know," I said. "We could try a dropper." I hurried into the house to find one. Earl sucked hungrily from the dropper and the eating problem was solved.

Step three was to choose an option and implement it. Earl stayed.

I know you're dying to know what happened to Earl, so I'll finish the story. Earl grew up to be a beautiful, healthy, bushy-tailed gray squirrel. We brought him nuts to hide before his first winter, and he went crazy storing them all over the yard and house.

Earl was like any ordinary squirrel except for the fact that he climbed people as if they were trees and made a nest in our garage. Earl left us one day and I'm afraid it was my fault. He and I got into a fight over a marshmallow. I know it sounds petty, but as a mother, I didn't think marshmallows were good for squirrels. Earl had other ideas and protested by sinking his front teeth into my forefinger.

I'd have forgiven him, but Earl apparently decided to give us up to raise his own family. We'd seen it coming even before the marshmallow incident. Earl had a girl. We lost track of him soon after that. Seems some neighbor chased him off, thinking any wild squirrel that would run straight up a man's pant leg had to be crazy or rabid.

Earl is long gone now, but we'll never forget him. In the backyard where he once buried an acorn, an oak tree lives and grows.

You may want to analyze problems of a more serious or complex nature on paper rather than in your head.

1. Write down the problem. Sometimes that helps bring it into focus and down to a smaller size.
2. Consider the problem from all angles and brainstorm for solutions.
3. Choose the most logical solution and act on it.
4. If your first option fails, reconsider and try again.
5. Pray as you go. There is no problem too big for God.

Teach Your Children Well

If our children are blank pages upon which we write their future, then we must carefully consider what we want to write.

Before we begin, we realize that the paper isn't quite blank, for God has already begun work in them. Our children are born with some natural abilities and gifts—it is our job to enhance those abilities and learn of those gifts.

I wanted to teach my children well. I wanted them to be successful, well-rounded, responsible adults. Maybe I could write the word *success* across the page in bright, bold letters.

But how do you spell *success?* Some mothers have been known to spell it M-O-N-E-Y. Others spell it D-R-E-A-M-S. I suppose all moms secretly desire financial comfort and career fulfillment for their children. Most of us wish our children would find the dream we have for them.

One day when my son was about seven, I noticed him playing doctor with his toy doctor kit. With plastic-rimmed glasses perched on his nose, he listened to his giant stuffed turtle's heart through the play stethoscope. I envisioned him in a black robe at graduation, having earned a medical degree from Harvard or Yale.

Success dreams for other mothers may include a new car every year and a home in the hills, with a maid. My son the doctor, my daughter the lawyer—those are success stories I may never see.

What I do see is the most important measure of success in my children. My kids' success isn't spelled M-O-N-E-Y. They don't have a lot of that yet.

But they do have hearts for helping others. They have a love for God. This is what I call success.

I guess if I had to write one word across my page it would be *success* spelled S-A-L-V-A-T-I-O-N.

12

The Throne Room

What a joy it is to have the opportunity to give our children the wealth of knowledge from a vault that never empties. Yet all the knowledge in the world is useless without the priceless crown from our next room.

Glass pedestals in varied shapes and sizes greet us as we enter. Atop each pedestal sits a crown—one from every royal head in the world. Hmmm . . . makes one feel rich just to look at them. How beautiful. They must be worth millions. Rubies, diamonds, sapphires, and emeralds—each crown seems more valuable than the next.

It would seem that all the wealth in the world is in this very room. But wait. Here in the back is a different sort of crown. It is encased in glass, as if to protect it. But isn't that only done to the most valuable pieces? The crown is made of twisted vine with hundreds of thorns as long and sharp as needles.

Beneath the crown of thorns is an inscription: "By this we know love, that He laid down His life for us."

Can there be a crown more precious than this? In terms of monetary value, it is priceless. It is a symbol of how much we are worth to God. It is a test of His love. He loved us enough to suffer and die so that we might live.

Love is a gift that can't be bought, only given.

And He Gave His Life

I once saw a film in which a Japanese man, a Christian, was riding on a train. As the train neared the top of the hill, the car in which he was riding became disengaged from the other cars.

The man, young and strong, with a sweetheart waiting for him at home, ran to the back of the car to assess the problem. The car sped faster and faster down the hill. There were no brakes and seemingly there was no way to stop the runaway car filled with terrified people. Women and children cried in anguish. If the train couldn't be stopped, they would all die.

The young man then realized there was only one way to stop the car. He jumped over the railing and threw himself on the track in front of the wheels. The train screeched to a halt as the wheels rammed into the young man's body.

"Greater love has no man than this, that a man lay down his life for his friends" (John 15:13 RSV).

His love and life were freely given.

Do You Really Love Your Children?

Love is "the will to extend one's self for the purpose of nurturing one's own or another's spiritual growth,"[1] says M. Scott Peck.

Do you really love your kids? Most parents will give you a look of surprise and say, "Of course."

It is easy enough to express love by simply saying the words out of habit or because we know we should. But love takes more than words. It is expressed in our actions—in how we feel about ourselves and others. Love takes a conscious effort and hard work.

Most of us have been duped into thinking that the warm, fuzzy sensation we get during a shared moment of intimacy is love. According to Peck, those are feelings and ". . . real love does not have its roots in feelings of love. On the contrary, real love often occurs in a context in which the feeling of love is lacking, when we act lovingly despite the fact that we don't feel loving."[2]

Emotions come and go, so real love must be based on something more tangible. Real love is based on a determined act of will.

It is easy enough to love an infant, who lies there in your arms and steals your heart away. For a while the babe is totally dependent on you. But what about later, maybe as the terrible twos come around, when the demands on your time and mind and body intensify, and your feelings of love are challenged—then what?

It is part of our natural maternal (parental) instinct to nurture. It takes work and courage (a giving up of ourselves or extending ourselves beyond the necessary) to turn our natural nurturing abilities into real love.

As our children grow, it becomes more difficult to love. Love consists of letting go and letting them grow independent from us. Out of fear we want to hang on—to protect them. Love is the courage to let go.

Love is being willing to take risks—saying no even at the risk of alienation, saying yes at the risk of hurt to yourself.

When I was a little girl in the postdepression days, there were times we had a shortage of food. Somehow I knew, though, that if there hadn't been enough food, my mother would have fed us before she fed herself.

I've never had to sacrifice my life or food for the sake of my children. I'm thankful for that, yet I can't help but wonder—would I step in front of my child to stop a bullet? Would I walk a hundred miles, like many African mothers, on an empty stomach, to find medical help and food for my child? Would I give my children the last morsel of bread?

I think I would. How about you? Most of our children are not in danger of starving physically, and most won't need us to sacrifice our lives to save theirs. But there are many children in our country who are starving—for time, for someone to listen, for discipline, for love, for a mom.

My good friend Marie attributes some of her frequent illnesses to her starvation for love and compassion as a child. "My mom was a perfectionist. At times I felt she was more a military sergeant than a mom. As I grew older I realized something, though. Whenever any of us was ill, she would stop demanding perfection from us and become loving and compassionate. I remember being sick a great deal as a child so that I could experience that warm, loving side of her."

How full of love are your children? Are you willing to give up part of yourself, your pleasure, your time for them?

Can you honestly say you love your child, no matter what he or she has done?

Jan, a mother of two, admitted that she couldn't love her son. "He's hurt me so much. He left home a few years ago without a word. He was gone for two years. I don't trust him. I can't . . . I just can't love him."

It isn't easy to love someone who has hurt you. Yet that is what unconditional love is all about. The Bible tells us to love those who hate us. When I'm tempted to deny love, I remember Jesus. After suffering and being tortured by His countrymen, He hung dying on the cross and whispered, "Father, forgive them." Then I think, no matter what anyone does to me, it won't hurt enough to stop my love.

Love like that filters into me from God. Love is activated and made unconditional by God. No matter how we try to explain it, there is a mystery we can't account for. I think it is because ultimately only God can instill in us what it takes to really love someone no matter what. For myself, it was through a conscious effort of loving God that I have been able to love myself and my children in an unconditional way.

An Attitude of Unconditional Love

There are several ways that can help you grow in an attitude of unconditional love.

I Yam What I Yam

There is a part of loving someone else that calls for us to accept our own and our children's unique and individual differences.

Remember the cartoon character Popeye? One of his most famous sayings was, "I yam what I yam." Popeye was unique. He was created by a cartoonist, and there is no other character like him.

No one has ever tried to change Popeye, because he is who he is. Yet many of us parents try to change our children. One of the most difficult things for some parents to accept is that we are all different. In fact, there can be extreme differences among family members.

In order to accept your child, it's important that you accept yourself. Accept yourself as a beautiful and unique person created by a loving Father, God. As you accept yourself, grow to accept your child—not as an extension of yourself, or a miniature you, but as a complete, separate person with unique talents and interests.

Each of us was created with a separate set of genes. And though most of our kids, even in grade school, opt for wearing the same kind of jeans, they really are different. A wise mother realizes that she hasn't necessarily failed as a mother when:

- She is meticulous, and her teenage daughter, Jenny, would rather write a story or paint a picture than clean the week's supply of dirty laundry off her bedroom floor.
- She is into gourmet cooking, and Jenny wouldn't know a hollandaise sauce from a roast duck.

135

- She lives for the evening news, and Jenny swoons over the latest teen idol and reads mystery novels.

While Mom doesn't and probably shouldn't accept Jenny's undisciplined behavior in leaving the laundry, she will want to be careful not to crush Jenny's special talents and unique character. Just because Jenny likes different things doesn't mean she's wrong. Acceptance defuses the drive to control.

Acceptance is harder when you are faced with children who make serious mistakes in life or who opt for different lifestyles, especially if those lifestyles openly defy your beliefs and morals.

As parents we can't and shouldn't accept wrongdoing. We have a responsibility to point out to our children what they've done or are doing wrong. We can hate what they've done but still love and accept them.

Acceptance is following Jesus' example. "While we were yet sinners Christ died for us." In our sinful state He loved and accepted us.

I have a method for accepting my kids that you might want to adopt. My children and I are all God's kids. When I am somewhat imperfect, I look to my Father, God, for forgiveness. Jesus covers for me so God only sees me as perfect. He sees me for what I can become as well as what I am. It's as though He puts on a special pair of glasses with Jesus as the lens.

It might help if, whenever we see our kids in situations we can't accept, we put on our *Jesus glasses* so we can see them as God does. By accepting our children, we move closer to our goal of unconditional love.

Shaping Up Your Attitude

How do you feel about your children? What is your heart attitude about rearing your kids? Do you look forward to being with them each day or do you find any possible excuse to get out of the house?

Years ago, when my children were six and eight, I decided to go back to school. I entered a nursing program and barely found time to eat and sleep. Studying took up most of my free time, and I began to see my family as an intrusion in my life.

I can't explain how it happened. I felt a perpetual guilt. Something was wrong, but I didn't stop to think it through. There simply wasn't time. I would frantically run home after classes or a clinical workday at the hospital, throw dinner together, and practically inhale it. Then I would give the kids their baths and hustle them off to bed.

I should have let them stay up, but what could I do? As long as they were still up, I couldn't study. Once they'd gone to bed, I stuffed my guilt into the recesses of my gray matter and hit the books until midnight. Morning dawned and I'd be up by six or before to get a start on the day.

Their constant nagging irritated and annoyed me. If someone had asked me the question "If you could live your life over again, would you have children?" I might have said no. Let's face it, I had developed a lousy attitude.

One night as I anxiously submitted to the good-night ritual of a prayer and a kiss, I glanced up at my two fresh-scrubbed babies. The shock waves lashed through me like a million lightning bolts. I felt as though I'd been in a time warp during those first few months of school and had been dumped out on the other side of childhood. My children were growing up. What had I missed? David was at least an inch taller. When was the last time we marked his height on the giraffe chart on his door? Caryl's front teeth were missing. Had the tooth fairy remembered to slip a reward under her pillow?

The guilt I'd been feeling was real. I gathered them into my arms, and through snuffles and tears, managed to tell them I was sorry.

Fortunately, the resentment I felt toward my family for being needy and keeping me from achieving my appointed goal subsided. I continued my studies and eventually got my degree, but I didn't want college so much that I'd risk hurting or losing my family. I only prayed I hadn't hurt my kids too badly by my brief encounter with neglect.

If I had it to do again, would I have children? Yes, if my attitude was such that I could enthusiastically accept the challenge and responsibility of parenting. Yes! Yes, regardless, because I couldn't imagine a world without David and Caryl.

Besides, I've learned the importance of having an attitude of love and of putting my children's needs before my own. Children should never ache inside for lack of love. They should never have empty arms with no one to fill them.

Have You Hugged Your Child Today?

Part of loving a child is showing that child how much you care by the use of outward affection.

"I need hugs and kisses from my mom," writes Dwight, age ten.

A sixteen-year-old girl said, "I don't think parents should stop hugging and kissing their kids just because they get a little older." Granted, many adolescents develop an allergy to hugs and kisses. Get near them with either and they're apt to break out in hives or disappear.

In my book *Have You Hugged Your Teenager Today?* I stressed the importance of showing love with hugs for kids of all ages—even when they insist you cool it. It isn't always feasible to wrestle a kid to the floor in order to execute your hug, as I have been known to do. Sometimes a back rub, a hand on the shoulder, a touch, or even just a smile, will be enough of a hug to say "I love you."

I persisted with showing my love in a physical way and it worked. Now my kids hug me. And guess what? I think they like it.

Forgiveness—a Crown of Glory

Perhaps the most important aspect of gaining unconditional love is being able to forgive and forget.

> The LORD says, "Do not cling to events of the past or dwell on what happened long ago. Watch for the new thing I am going to do. It is happening already—you can see it now! I will make a road through the wilderness and give you streams of water there."
>
> Isaiah 43:18–19 TEV

Within a family unit, we can expect a lot of hurts. At times we may see an unceasing parade of harsh words and actions. Unforgiveness harbors resentments and the opening and reopening of old wounds. The wounds fester and cause a decaying that can eventually rot away the foundation of the family.

The only way healing can take place is through forgiveness.

We seem to be built with an inner voice that counsels us to forgive and forget. Sometimes we rush in to say we're sorry and express platitudes to make certain we've done the "right" thing. In teaching our children, we may rush in to right the wrong by insisting on an immediate apology.

Six-year-old Tommy rushes into the house screaming. "Mom! Casey hit me!"

"I did not, you big baby!" Casey yells. "Mom, he tore down my Lego house."

"I did not, I tripped."

"That's not true, Mom. He kicked it."

"I did not!"

"Did too!"

Mother resists the urge to knock their heads together and calmly pulls the boys apart. "Stop your arguing. Tommy, tell Casey you're sorry for knocking over his house, and Casey, apologize to Tommy for hitting him. Come on now, boys, shake hands and make up."

The boys will probably give in to Mom's demand. They will squelch their anger—for now—and pretend it's over. But is it really forgiveness? Will the unresolved conflict simmer below the surface, only to rise full force in another storm?

Forgiveness happens when the past is turned loose and relationships are resolved and restored. Forgiveness frees us to love, live, and trust again.

Perhaps it would be better for Mom to separate Tommy and Casey until the anger passes, then let them talk out their misunderstanding and help them come to a resolution.

Forgiveness is never easy, and it can take a long time for the pain and guilt to go away. But I think we must make the effort—to take the first step toward forgiving—even if we fall along the way.

David Augsburger, in his book *Caring Enough to Forgive,* says:

> We must not refuse to move toward another in seeking mutual repentance and renewed trust.
>
> Yet we cannot despair of forgiveness and lose hope that reconciliation is possible.
>
> So let us forgive as gently and genuinely as is possible in any situation of conflict between us.
>
> So let us forgive as fully and as completely as we are able in the circumstances of our misunderstandings.
>
> So let us reach out for reconciliation as openly and authentically as possible for the levels of maturity we have each achieved.
>
> So let us forgive freely, fully, at times even foolishly, but with all the integrity that is within us.[3]

Let's look again at the crown of thorns displayed in this room of priceless treasure. It is a symbol of unconditional love, of giving, and it is also the symbol of forgiveness. It was for our sake—that we could be forgiven—that Christ wore the crown and died.

In forgiveness, we teach our children by our actions. It is never a sign of weakness to admit when you're wrong or to forgive someone who has hurt you, even when that someone is your child.

Kids need a mom who knows the essence of forgiveness and who instills that quality in her children. In order for a family to even have a chance at unity, forgiveness must play an intricate part in their way of life.

With acceptance, an improved attitude, hugs and kisses, and forgiveness, you should be well on your way to displaying that unconditional love we talked about at the beginning of this chapter.

"A mom," my daughter once told me, "is someone who has to love you no matter what you do."

Do you?

As we make our way down the hall, let's not close love's door. Leave it open so love can filter through the whole house.

13

The Servant's Quarters

There is only one more key to try. This door swings open more easily than the others. But the room is practically bare. Off to one side I see a cushion on the floor. Before it stands a low altar adorned only with a rustic wooden cross, a single candle, and a Bible.

In front of the window sits a pitcher and a bowl with a washcloth and towel draped over a small bench. Have we opened the wrong door? This is supposed to be filled with the most valuable treasure of all. When I first discovered the key to this room, I felt I'd made a mistake. I went back out into the hallway and checked the door again. On it, in letters almost too faded to see, was written SERVANT'S QUARTERS.

There had been no mistake. It was the only room left to explore and the only key left in my hand. Eventually, as years passed, I came to understand. The few simple elements in this room symbolized the tools of a mother's trade.

Let's examine first the element of serving—the pitcher and bowl. They are symbolic of servanthood. Perhaps you will remember the scene in the Bible where Jesus knelt and washed His disciples' feet. He gave them an example to follow. William Barclay, in his Bible study series, interprets the incident in this way:

At that r
had sup
example
form th
Someti
humble
was no
His dis

My fir
thing lik
let my ki
slave to
life, I sa

There are times when it takes a
our job as a mother. Such was t
Julie is a divorced, workin
back home after a long da
mood for her two kids,
day had gone as so
that morning, and
cow.
She grum
put your
living
as

Help Wanted . . . Professional Mom.

If you were to run an advertisement for a mom, your ad
might look something like this:

WANTED: Mother. Salary: $00. No retirement, no insurance,
no guarantees. Bonuses for a job well done may include a few
hugs and kisses. Skills required: Must love children, cats, dogs,
hamsters, and fish. Must be able to cook peanut butter and
jelly sandwiches and chocolate chip cookies and other good
stuff. Must like to drive a car full of kids to the zoo. Must have
nursing experience for kissing owies, and lots of bandages.
Must be able to love a kid, even when he's rotten. . . .

It's slave labor, right? Why do we do it? Well . . . because.
Sometimes it's a terrific, satisfying, and even fun job. Nothing tugged at my motherly heartstrings more than those times
when I

- . . . watched my baby nurse contentedly in my arms.
- . . . tenderly brushed aside a tangle of curls from the moist
  brow of a sleeping child.

little longer to appreciate
the case with Julie.

mom. One day as she trudged
y at the office, she was not in the
Daniel, age four, and Kim, three. The
r as the milk she'd left on the counter
Julie felt about as cranky as an unmilked

bled at her kids. "Oh . . . why can't you kids ever
toys away? And Daniel, you left your shoes in the
oom again." She hovered dangerously close to tears
e surveyed the mess.

"Mom?" Daniel started to ask his four hundred and fifti-
eth question since she'd picked them up at the sitter's.

Without giving him a chance to finish she snapped, "If you
call me *Mom* one more time, I'll send you to your room without supper."

Daniel ran into his room sobbing, and guilt hovered over
her like a hawk, talons outstretched, swooping in for the
kill.

Julie sighed deeply and sank into the nearest chair. She
wondered why she had ever decided to have kids in the first
place. "All I ever do is give, give, give. But do I ever get anything in return?" Right in the middle of her pity party, two
small arms crept around her neck from behind and a gentle whisper chased away all her regrets. "I still love you,
Mommy."

At times, as with any job, mothering can be a thankless
position. But being a servant mom doesn't mean we have to
do everything or be Super Mom. We've already seen the perils of such folly. But it may mean putting some of our plans
on hold while we help our children grow up. It may mean
spending time serving in the Mom Corps.

Maybe nobody would answer an ad for the job of being a
mother, but if a mother doesn't do it, who will?

Above and Beyond the Call of Duty

Not only doesn't the job of mothering pay very well, but mothers get no respect. Chances are, we won't be noticed or appreciated as we carry out the job of mothering. Few mothers are ever decorated for valor in providing services above and beyond the call of duty. Yet above and beyond is exactly what we are called to do.

Although we won't often receive recognition or praise for many of our behind-the-scenes duties, that's no reason to feel discouraged. We've been led, by advertisers and marketing specialists, to expect more out of life than an occasional "Thanks, Mom," or "I love you."

Perhaps a modern mother's dream is to waltz into the dining room with a full-course dinner and actually have someone notice that she used a polyunsaturated oil instead of bacon grease.

And what mother wouldn't smile while cleansing the toilet bowl as her wide-eyed little cherub gazed over her shoulder in amazement at the white tornado magically swooshing through the grime?

Do you think kids really care if their clothes feel snuggly soft and smell like fabric softener? And how many kids have you met recently who would say, "Oh, look, the plates are so shiny I can see myself," as they set the table (without complaint) for dinner?

This is the real world, Mom. A place where kids move too fast to smell clean underwear along the way. If we're lucky, they'll notice that we've sorted and folded their clean clothes and neatly laid them on their beds. If we're lucky, they'll put them in their drawers, rather than let them fall to the floor as they absently throw back the covers. If we're lucky, they won't stay on the floor, only to be scooped up a week later, never worn, to be laundered again.

There are many things we mothers do for which we'll never get recognition, such as washing 6,200 diapers in a single year, or kissing 102 owies to make them all better. But didn't Jesus say, ". . . whoever would be great among you must be your servant . . . even as the Son of man came not to be served but to serve, and to give his life as a ransom for many" (Matt. 20:26–28 RSV)?

However, this doesn't mean we are to indulge ourselves in all the behind-the-scenes jobs around the house. If you are doing too many things that go unnoticed or unappreciated, perhaps your children aren't doing enough. I firmly believe children should be given an equal share in household chores. We wouldn't want to keep them from receiving their reward in heaven, would we?

I have always been an equal-opportunity-employment mother. By providing the kids with a map and simple instructions, I made sure my children could find their way to the laundry room, bathrooms, and kitchen during cleaning time.

At first, handing the tasks I had religiously hoarded for years over to my kids wasn't easy. I suffered pangs of jealousy and selfishness. I wanted to keep the joys of motherhood all to myself. "They can't do the job as well as I can," I mused. Finally, I gave in. After all, I reasoned, my mother had always taught me to share.

So what if the towels weren't always perfectly folded or a red shirt occasionally tinted all the white clothes pink—I had to think of the children.

As a mother, how could I deny a child the thrill of washing dishes, clothing, floors, and bathrooms? Could you withhold from a child the adventure of attacking dust, armed with only a can of Pledge and a dustcloth?

It's possible that your child won't agree with your unselfish act. Perhaps the word *can't* will become the new four-letter word in your kid's vocabulary. For times like this you may want to brush up on quick comebacks like:

"That's tough."

"Dirt and Ty-D-Bol wait for no man."

"Life is hard."

Naturally, as children share in the tasks, they also need to learn what it's like not to be awarded a medal for everything. A child should learn what it feels like to spend hours cleaning the kitchen, only to have it messed up again at the next meal.

A kid needs a mother who will allow the child to learn what it takes to keep a household running (not necessarily smoothly—just running).

As children learn to serve by helping out around the house, they can learn some valuable lessons, such as:

- Life is not necessarily fair.
- Helping out leaves more time for Mom to have fun with the kids.
- Work is easier when you share the load.
- Serving (giving) can be fun.

Be careful, however. If your children are included in the family work force, they *may* come to appreciate what you do for them.

Being a servant involves more than just doing a job that nobody else wants, or teaching your children by letting them serve.

You've Come a Long Way, Baby

The idea of servanthood covers our entire way of life. It means to set aside all selfish desires and focus not on yourself but on the needs of others. I have to admit that submission, humility, and the idea of being least have gotten some bad publicity of late.

This teaching of counting others better than myself could get me in trouble with many, perhaps even a majority, of women today. I've heard that if I want to move up in the world I must think of myself. I've got to look out for Number One because if I don't look out for me, who will?

But when I focus too long on me, on my rights, on what's best for Mommy, to the exclusion of my children, I feel . . . I don't know . . . off balance. Does that make sense? I think it's because that's not the way God wants me to be.

Being a servant mother doesn't mean getting walked on, or never doing things for ourselves.

Serving means giving encouragement, love, compassion, tenderness, and comfort to our children and others (Phil. 2:1).

Serving means to "do nothing from selfishness or conceit, but in humility count others better than yourselves" (Phil. 2:3 RSV).

Serving means we must "look not only to [our] own interests, but also to the interests of others" (Phil. 2:4 RSV).

Interestingly enough, it is that servantlike attitude I use as a nurse in dealing with my patients. Patients are important, but aren't children even more so?

A servant's attitude should be the same as Christ's, "who, though he was in the form of God, did not count equality with God a thing to be grasped, but emptied himself, taking the form of a servant . . ." (Phil. 2:6–7 RSV).

Now maybe you're wondering how to apply this idea of servanthood in your family. Here's a suggestion:

Take out the basin and pitcher, or better yet, just use a little baby oil. Now, ask one of your kids to take off his shoes and socks (then make him wash his feet). Ready? Massage his feet with the warmed oil, about five minutes per foot. Chances are (unless you kept him from an important game or something) the foot massage will have him ready to obey your every command.

Actually, all kidding aside, washing or massaging another person's feet breaks down pride on both sides. It's an intimate, loving gesture. And, oh . . . does it feel good.

My understanding of the benefits of becoming a servant-like mother came at about the same time I realized the need for God in my life.

Things Go Better with God

As I grew and developed as a mother, I came to realize one important fact: Without God, I could never have survived mothering.

Oh, I know there are skeptics out there who would laugh at me for saying that, but it's true. In my children's earlier years, although I believed in God, I didn't really know I could lean on Him when times got tough. I thought if I tried hard enough I could eventually become the kind of mother my psychology books and Mother's Day cards told me I should be.

In the beginning of my time as a mother, I was like a delicate pink rosebud—fresh, innocent, with all the fragrant ideals of motherhood stored inside me. I stood ready to burst into bloom. I (even though others before me never seemed to quite make it) would be the perfect Mother Rose.

As I held my first child in my arms and watched him hungrily search for milk, I was even more convinced I could reach my goal. My son, David, needed me, and I wasn't about to let him down.

The first few months went beautifully. My petals glowed with health and happiness. Then my adorable baby boy began to crawl (into everything), and my life hasn't been the same since.

As my expectations collapsed, so did my strength. Just as David turned two, our second child was born. I should have known there'd be trouble. Caryl didn't particularly want to leave her cozy amniotic sac and took two weeks to make up her mind.

In spite of the difficulties I'd been encountering, I vowed (as she lay curled up beside me) that I could still be a fantastic mother.

I tried. I failed. Caryl turned out to be a colicky baby. Naturally I blamed myself. What was I doing wrong? Failure to comfort her led to irritation, frustration, angry words, and tears. I wanted to scream—to send her back. Mothers weren't supposed to feel that way.

A petal wilted—crushed by false hopes and expectations.

I vowed my children and I would survive the terrible twos together. We did, but not without a few fights. The bumps and thumps and no's added up to one great big emotional bruise for their mom.

More petals fell and drifted to the floor in defeat.

On the outside I pretended to be smooth and perfectly balanced. And with a few petals missing, that wasn't an easy task. I walked, talked, and acted like a good mother should. No one knew of the confusion and hurt I felt as the thorns along my sides seemed to turn inward to pierce my flesh. No one guessed the dew that clung to my petals in the morning light had been tears from the long night before.

By the time my children were eight and ten, all pretense was gone. I had failed. The perfect-mother image took a nose dive as I sat in the pew of our church one Sunday morning and glanced at my "well groomed" son. Shock ricocheted through my body. How could I have missed it? He'd looked absolutely dashing when we left the house. But now . . . from under his neatly pressed suit pants peeked the ragged hem of an old pair of jeans . . . and below that . . . (gasp) tennis shoes. Tucked under his white shirt and tie I could make out the plaid of an old, frayed flannel shirt.

"Why?" I asked him.

F
an
rea
(
my
(
It ju
mo
mot
N
and
toge
as a
A
Goo
mak
wha

I'd deserted Him. He had every right to turn me down.

I'd made a mess of things and didn't think even God could want me now. But even as I thought it through, God had begun working to restore me. I still had a family who needed me and in spite of everything, I loved them. I wasn't ready to give up, so I prayed a very simple prayer. I just said, "God, help!"

God, like a Master Gardener, nurtured my roots with the living water of His Word. He pruned away the dead stems and blossoms, fertilized me with truth, and restored me to life.

A kid needs a mom who needs God. I am a better mother (not perfect) because I live in the strength God gives me. I love my children because He first loved me, as I have expressed in this poem.

> He gives me hope in hopeless situations,
> And helps me see the rainbow
> On the other side of rain.
> He heals the thorn-infested wounds
> That I might smell the roses.

...ne pain;

...gh again.

...have done one thing right, it
...ren the truth of needing and lov-

...ieved in Me"

...re is yet another part of being a servant mother.
...member the cushion and altar in the room marked SER-
VANT'S QUARTERS? I spent a lot of time praying for my children. By praying for them, I believed God would hear my
prayers and give me the faith I needed to believe in them.

"Mom," my daughter, Caryl, once said, "the most important thing you ever did as a mother was to believe in me."

I did and do believe in my children. I wish I could say I
never doubted whether or not they'd even survive their teenage years. My children weren't aware of most of the doubts,
or that it was God working through me who managed to keep
me believing everything would work out. In the bleakest
moments, when I paced the floor at night wondering if I'd
ever see my runaway teenage son again, it was my belief and
faith in God that allowed me to see beyond the past and present into a hopeful future. God's promises gave me the strength
to hold on—promises such as: "Weeping may endure for a
night, but joy comes in the morning" (Ps. 30:5 NKJV) and "All
things work together for good to those who love God" (Rom.
8:28 NKJV).

In my weakness I learned how to lean on God to regain
my strength and know that His grace was sufficient for me.
When I realized He held the controls in my children's lives,
believing in them became easy again.

I don't believe my children are infallible and will never make mistakes. But I do believe they are in God's hands. As my paraphrase of Isaiah 43:1–3 says:

The LORD has called them by name, they are His. When they pass through the waters He will be with them; and through the rivers, they shall not overwhelm them; when they walk through fire they shall not be burned, and the flame shall not consume them. For He is the LORD their God, the Holy One of Israel, their Savior.

How can I be so sure of these biblical promises?

"It's a Miracle, Mom"

A few years ago, we received a call from the police in Montana.

"We've found a pickup your son was traveling in—totaled. It had been driven over a cliff and David's trunk was found near the wreck. We found a lot of blood in the truck and around it, but no sign of your son or the boy he was with."

For four days I had no idea whether my son was alive or dead. I had nowhere to turn but to the Lord. I spent my days in constant prayer. On the fourth day he called home. He and his friend had been on the run, since the truck had been stolen. David had reached the end of his rope and needed our help. We told him to come home. His ordeal prompted him to turn his life around. In telling us his story he said, "It was a miracle, Mom. People get killed in crashes like that, but all we got were a few cuts and bruises." *When they walk through the fire they shall not be burned.*

Children need a mother who realizes their potential and helps them believe they can achieve it—even if some of her believing power comes from a higher source.

Sometimes a mother's world seems dark and cold. If you are a mother who lives in shades of darkness, come back into the room. Remember the candle on the altar? Light it.

Now, kneel on the cushion and ask Jesus to come into your heart and be the light of your world. Then keep the candle lit in the altar of your heart as a remembrance. Whenever darkness closes in, look at that candle and know . . . that all the darkness in the world can't put out this single light.

Part 3

What's a Mother to Do?

We've finished touring the mansion within a mother's heart. Were you surprised at the resources you found there? I hope you didn't find the treasure house of better mothering too exhausting, or worse, too depressing. So often, when we start talking about how to become better mothers, we end up with terminal guilt.

If you're feeling a bit overwhelmed right now, relax—you're not alone. I've talked to so many mothers lately who are frustrated, depressed, guilt ridden, and dissatisfied—in their spare time.

Both moms who are employed outside the home and moms who stay home suffer from unhappiness and instability. "I don't know what's wrong," said one young mother. "It just feels like something's missing from my life."

So often in our fast-paced world, we lose sight of who and what we are. In his book *What Kids Need Most in a Dad*, Tim Hansel quoted another father: "I feel so often like I'm having an identity crisis and an energy crisis at the same time. I don't know who I am and I don't have the energy to find out."

Kids need a mom who knows herself and can be satisfied—even delighted—in the role or roles she plays.

Are you happy with your lot in life, or would you rather be sailing? In the next few chapters we'll be doing just that—not sailing, but helping you get in touch with yourself and how you really feel about what you do. First, however, let's take a quick look at the vast network of different lifestyles that make up today's moms.

More than 50 percent of today's moms are employed in jobs outside the home. Some mothers work outside the home because finances dictate they must. Some work away because they want to. Some would rather stay home in their job as homemaker/wife/ mother. Some pursue their careers or run businesses from their homes.

Mothers come from varied backgrounds, but most of us share a common goal: We want to do a good job of mothering our kids.

In the next chapter we'll talk about moving into a satisfied, happier life, determining your purpose, and reestablishing priorities.

In chapter 15 you'll find valuable helps for working moms such as throwing off the yoke of guilt, helping children adjust to and accept Mom working, child-care alternatives, and sharing the load.

Chapter 16 will include helps for stay-at-home moms. We'll discuss topics such as overcoming social pressures, how to avoid the dangers of staying home, changing times, and dealing with isolation and loneliness.

In chapter 17 we'll talk about the seasons of a mother's life.

14

Mama Said There'd Be Days like This

Today's moms are different from moms of even a generation ago. Demands on mothers have risen to dangerous proportions. Even mothers, when overloaded, can short-circuit and self-destruct.

Especially when your day goes like this:

It is 6:00 A.M. Susan (I'll name her that, but she could be any one of you) manages to drag herself out of bed. Her husband, George, grabs the back of her silk nightie, flashes her an irresistible smile, and says, "Why don't you come back to bed for a few minutes, sweetheart?"

Half an hour later Susan hauls herself out of bed again. This time George pats her on the behind and says, "How's about a big breakfast this morning, honey?"

"Sure thing," Susan promises. At that moment she'd promise him the moon, carved into bite-sized pieces. He's her husband, friend, and lover, and she's his willing servant. "Go back to sleep for about an hour," she croons. "I'll wake you with breakfast in bed."

She hums an old familiar love song as she dreamily shuffles down the hall and into the kitchen, then dutifully tosses hubby's bacon into a pan.

"Mom!" her daughter Janelle screams. "You're not ready."

"Shhh. You'll wake your father. Ready for what?"

"Don't tell me you forgot. I told you to set the alarm early so you could take me to rally squad practice this morning. Mom," Janelle moans. "I have to be there by six-thirty."

"Oh, honey, I'm sorry."

"Sorry? If I'm late I could get kicked off the squad. My life will be ruined, and all you can say is, 'I'm sorry'?"

"Oh . . . here." Susan pushes the car keys at her teenage daughter. "Go start the car. I won't bother to dress. I'll just throw a coat over my robe. It's only a few minutes away and no one will see me." Susan jams the bacon into the oven and turns it up to four hundred degrees. It will be done to perfection by the time she gets back.

As Susan heads back home a few minutes later, she smiles at her flexibility. Even though she had to rush Janelle to school, it won't interrupt her morning.

With only four blocks to go, Susan glances in her rearview mirror, only to be confronted by red-and-blue flashing lights. A yowling siren tells her to pull over.

By the time Susan drives into her driveway and dashes into the house, smoke has filled the kitchen and is drifting down toward the . . .

Be-e-e-e-e-! The sound of the smoke alarm brings the rest of her household to life.

"Don't you know better than to leave bacon unattended? You could have killed us all with that stupid trick . . . ow!" George mutters as he burns his hand on the fire-blackened pan. Susan listens to another five minutes of George's rantings about fire hazards as they open windows and doors to clear the air.

"I'm hungry," Ryan, age six, complains.

"Mom." A voice belonging to twelve-year-old Kim rings up the stairway. "Where are my gym clothes—you were supposed to wash them last night."

"Susan," George bellows, "where's my blue tie? I asked you to pick it up at the cleaner's yesterday."

"Mom, I can't find my science book."

"Mommy, I'm hungry."

The voices become a blur of endless demands and Susan . . . well, Susan's curled up in a little ball under her covers—the electric blanket turned up high—wishing she were a little girl so she could suck her thumb again.

Come on, be honest now. Aren't there days when you can see yourself running around in circles, crying, "This does not compute," like a robot with a few essential screws loose?

What Went Wrong?

As we look in on Susan a little later, we find that she's finally crawled out of her warm, safe cocoon, but she isn't happy. "Why couldn't I have handled the morning better? If only I'd remembered why I set the alarm." The craziness of the morning wouldn't have been so bad in itself—if it had been the first time. But it hadn't. Susan hurries to get herself in order before her friend Karen arrives. *I may be a hassled, half-crazed homemaker,* she says to herself, *but at least I can still pretend that all is well. Can't I?*

After all, Karen owns and manages a small boutique at the mall, is rearing four well-behaved kids, keeps a clean house, and reads at least two novels a week. And she does it all alone. Her husband left town on business with a very young, very attractive, very successful female attorney five years ago and never came back. In spite of all that, Karen finds time to be a loving and supportive friend.

How would it look if I told her I couldn't even manage a simple breakfast? Susan pastes on a smile. She doesn't like playing the game, but what can she do? There are no smiles left inside of her.

As the doorbell rings and Karen hugs her in greeting, Susan's facade crumbles as tears betray her.

"Susan." Karen ushers her now sobbing friend to the sofa. "What's wrong?"

The words of explanation over the morning crisis spill out and mingle with the flow of tears.

Karen sits quietly, just listening. When her friend finishes her tale of woe, she says, "Oh, Sue, it must have been terrible, but we all have days like that. C'mon, let's go shopping. That will cheer you up."

"No, it's no use. I've been having too many days like this." Susan stands and walks to the fireplace. "You see this picture? Our family portrait. I was so confident then, so sure . . . oh, Karen, what's the use? I'm a failure. I keep thinking I should be doing something different. I've even thought of leaving my family. I'm not much good to them anyway."

"Susan, you're a wonderful mother and wife. How can you say that?"

"Well, it's true. I don't even know who I am anymore, or why I was born. I sometimes wish I'd never met George or had the children . . . oh." Susan holds a tissue to her face to catch another stream of tears. "There, you see? I'm a terrible mother . . . how could I even think things like that?"

"Because you're normal." Karen wraps a comforting arm across Susan's shoulders. "Listen, I know exactly what you're going through. It's a crisis most mothers find themselves in at some time or other."

"It is? How would you know? You always seem so together . . ."

"I always was a great actress."

"Really?"

"Really. I'll tell you what. Go wash your face, fix your makeup, and I'll take you out for coffee and a delectable piece of amaretto fudge cake. Then I'll show you a secret to beat the blues on a permanent basis."

Are You Riding in a Rut?

Since the secret Karen was going to share with Susan was one I shared with Karen, I'm going to pause here to bring you all a little closer to the fire.

Probably the most valuable insight I learned as a mother is the art of being happy. The way I see it, we have two roads on which to travel through life. One road leads us in the groove of happiness and satisfaction, and the other bumps us along in ruts of sadness and despair.

Most of us do a little bouncing back and forth between the two. The secret of happy mothering is knowing which road to take.

Which road are you traveling on? To help you determine that, I'd like you to take a short quiz.

	True	False
1. I experience a lot of frustration these days.	[ ]	[ ]
2. I'm not very happy with my job.	[ ]	[ ]
3. I feel as if I'm off target with my life.	[ ]	[ ]
4. Mothering isn't what I hoped it would be.	[ ]	[ ]
5. I feel as if I'm losing control.	[ ]	[ ]
6. I often feel isolated and stranded in my situation.	[ ]	[ ]
7. I try so hard and can't seem to get ahead.	[ ]	[ ]
8. Sometimes I think my kids would be better off with someone else to mother them.	[ ]	[ ]
9. I need a change, but I don't know what to do.	[ ]	[ ]
10. There are too many demands on my time, and sometimes I feel like running away from it all.	[ ]	[ ]
11. Sometimes I feel trapped in my circumstances.	[ ]	[ ]
12. When I see how others are coping, I get more depressed.	[ ]	[ ]

These are just a few of many questions I could ask, but these twelve should be enough for you to determine your present direction. If most of your answers were *true*, then chances are you are in a rut and heading for more gloom. If you ended up with more *false* answers, you're probably meandering a little closer to happiness.

Our friend Susan was definitely heading down the grinding road of dissatisfaction. Karen, on the other hand, had once been in the same rut, but had managed to climb over to the other side. Her walk along life's way is smoother, easier, and all-around more pleasant. How did Karen make the transfer to happier mothering?

She did it simply by learning more about the roads, where they lead, and what she could do to change her course.

Let's take a look now at the two roads I described.

The Road to the Pits	*The Road to Satisfaction*
1. Focus on self and problems—a complainer	1. Focus on God
2. Low self-esteem	2. High self-esteem
3. Lack of vision or goals	3. Vision (goals)
4. Feelings of uselessness, unworthiness	4. Accomplishments (feels useful)
5. Sense of hopelessness	5. Hope—excitement for tomorrow
6. Fear of new things/ inflexibility	6. Flexibility—eagerness to learn
7. Insecurity	7. Security in position
8. Stagnation	8. Growth and learning
9. Depression/stress/anxiety	9. Vitality
10. Problems never end	10. Problem solver

When Susan answered the questions she said, "Oh, great. I'm riding straight down to the dumps. So what do I do now? How can you expect me to change places? I'm using all the strength I have to just hold on so I don't fall off."

Changing your position isn't easy, but it is possible. I found myself in much the same position Susan was in. One of the first steps for me was to determine my purpose in life.

Why Was I Born?

Part of the unrest felt by mothers today, whether they've chosen a career that takes them outside the home or one that allows them to work at home, is that they haven't discovered their purpose in life.

Do you find yourself asking questions like these:

"Why was I born?"

"Is that all there is?"

"What's the use?"

Or have you made statements like this one:

"I've considered all the options, and there's only one way out. I'm running away from home."

The trouble is, even if you chose to run away from it all, you'd still be traveling down the same lonely highway, sloshing through mud and disillusionment.

If you feel as if you may have taken a wrong turn, here are some questions and answers that can help you make the change.

1. What is your relationship with God? Chances are, if you've taken the windy path to gloom and doom, you've lost sight of God in your life. If you'll check the list again, you'll find that on the happiness road I've written about focusing on God. When we keep ourselves focused on God and walk the course He sets for us, we can never stay in misery for long. There is no problem too big for us if we keep God as the central point in our lives.

2. Why were you born? What a question. Theologically, I could say, "We were all born to do the will of God." While the message is basically true, to leave it at that would be a simple way out. I believe each of us was born for a purpose. Some-

times it takes a lifetime of trial and error to find what that purpose is. The next few questions may help you find the answers.

3. What are your gifts and special talents? Each of us is like a weaving, made up of many threads. There is one main fiber that is woven through me. It reflects, like sparks of gold, in everything I do. I'm an artist. As a mother, I spent a lot of time teaching my children how to create.

I became a nurse because another of my strongest fibers is compassion and seeing the best in people.

Make a list of what you most like to do, then choose one or two favorites. That is probably your specialty.

4. What would God want you to accomplish in your lifetime? Not an easy question for anyone. I can't predict the future, but I can be willing to try anything once. I have an open-door policy where God is concerned. If I'm not sure which way to go, I simply try all the doors available. If they open, I walk through. If not—I don't. Maybe I'll get my fingers smashed in the process, but if I don't try, how will I know what God wants for me?

Many years ago I said, "God, I really want to serve you. Show me how." A door opened that led to being a writer. I stood on the threshold. Behind me was familiar territory. I was a potter and a nurse, and I certainly had enough to do without taking on whatever lay behind this new door. It was scary. I'd never been there before. Maybe it wasn't God, I thought. But how would I know unless I tried? I walked through the door and said, "Okay, God. You win." Today I'm an author, and I love it. This is God's will for me.

Look back over your life and write down the things you have already accomplished. Then look to the future in anticipation of more. Don't be afraid to try doors. Trust that God will close those He doesn't want you to go through.

5. How can you best use your talents to serve God? My talents are used when I write, sing, or speak for groups. When you submit yourself as a vessel for God's use, He decides how. All you have to do is say yes.

6. What is your responsibility to your family? When talents, accomplishments, and all the other good things you do get in the way of your relationships with your family, it's time to back off and take another look. Sometimes it's the church or religion that is asking for your time and talent—not God. Because my specific work in God's will involves writing, I don't involve myself in church socials or bazaars—it's not my job right now. I've learned to say no to many time-stealers because I need to write and, more important, spend time with my family.

7. Are you accomplishing God's will in your life? I've learned a great way to tell whether or not I'm in God's will. As a potter, I take a ball of clay and center it on the wheel. I gently assert my will and move it until it is where I want it. When it is centered, I can close my eyes and feel as if the clay and I are one. We move in perfect unison and I can even feel the quiet cooperation in my soul. It reminds me of how I as clay must be centered in God's will. I wrote a poem to describe my feelings at this marvelous discovery.

The Master Potter
He is the Potter, I am clay
He holds me in His hand—centers me—encircles me.
Like clay, I am weak and shapeless without the sustaining
    power of the Potter's hand.
If I resist, my life becomes turmoil . . . my impurities over-
    whelm me.
If I submit, He takes control. He opens me—molds me . . .
I begin to take shape and form.
I am real, full of life in His Holy Spirit.
Then again, if I resist, I become weak—I may break
For my walls are thin and transparent as the finest porcelain.
I must submit—returned to the whole, with wounds healed
    to remind me of my suffering:
And the perfect, life-restoring God, who salvages me.

When I'm off center—out of God's will—I feel restless, unsure. When that happens I have to take an accounting of my priorities and what I'm doing that doesn't coincide with God's will.

8. Are you willing to change if God wants you to shift priorities? Change isn't easy. I had to change from nursing to writing. I didn't want to at first, but God's gentle centering maneuvered me into a spot where I looked back one day and realized it had happened. But I had been willing to be moved.

My friend Sally is thrilled with being a stay-at-home mother. Her own children are grown now, but she likes the idea so much she's going to start all over again. She's adopting three children from El Salvador. Now *that* will be a full-time job.

"I'm a stay-at-home mom. It's what I do best, and I want to do it all my life," says Sally.

Yet in talking to Sally, I find a woman who is not necessarily locked into the role of the stay-at-home mom. She is versatile. She has worked off and on in special jobs, usually counseling, which she knows the Lord has called her to do. Some of her work has been on a volunteer basis; some has not.

While the children remain a higher priority than any job, she remains flexible.

9. Do you have a vision? The Bible says that "where there is no vision, the people perish" (Prov. 29:18 KJV). I see a lot of families perishing and wonder if lack of vision or purpose isn't part of the problem. Think about it. What do you want for your children? Your husband? And what do you want for yourself? Maybe part of the reason for your frustration as a mom is that you don't see beyond motherhood. Or maybe you have and it worries you.

In chapter 16 we'll work a little more on developing a vision for you not only as a mom but as an individual as well.

10. What are your goals or visions? As a mother, my vision was to see my children through childhood and watch them grow into responsible Christian adults. My vision has become a reality.

But I'm not just a mother. I have another vision for me. Because the children are grown I see this vision more clearly now. I decided to go back to school and get my master's degree.

Write down your goals, visions, hopes, and dreams. Keep the list in your diary or Bible and look at it periodically.

By moving onto the right road, finding a purpose, and having a vision, you are well on your way to being more satisfied and accepting of who and where you are.

Kids need a mom who can be happy and well adjusted whatever her situation, who, like the apostle Paul, has "learned, in whatever state I am, to be content" (Phil. 4:11 RSV). The wise mom accepts the things she can't change and works to change the things she can.

It isn't always easy to change directions. But goal setting, hard work, and prayer can help you make giant steps toward the path you were meant to follow. Sometimes we have to come back to the beginning and revise old habits and thought patterns.

It can be a frustrating experience to find yourself back at the starting place after years of work, but try not to think of the past, only of the bright new future that lies on the path you've chosen. It's time to burst forth and conquer new horizons in this new and exciting world of ours.

A good place to start over is by redefining priorities. Every once in a while, when I start feeling off center, I have to reevaluate my life and reset my priorities.

Priority Living

Have you ever come across the priority list for mothers? I've seen it in daily planning books and in various Bible-study programs. It goes something like this:

1. God (developing and maintaining a personal relationship through daily devotions and prayer)

2. Husband (if still in the home, being a helpmate to him, fitting into his plans)
3. Family (children, self, extended family)
4. People (church, neighbors, the world)
5. Job (employment, ministry)

I tend to agree with most of the list—to a point—but I see three problems. First, some women tend to take it too literally. Second, priorities change. And third, the number five priority, a job, may at times be intertwined with number one—your relationship with God.

There are times when a child becomes first priority. For example, say your ten-year-old falls out of an apple tree. As he's sprawled out on the ground, do you check your priority list to make sure you've placed God first and your husband second? Of course not. While you may stop to say a brief prayer, your priority will be to get that kid some help . . . fast.

Maybe you're saying, "Well, of course. That kind of priority shift is obvious." True, but let's move on to a little more drastic shift.

Some of the things at the bottom of your priority list may at times wind up near the top. What if your husband is injured and loses his job? You suddenly find yourself working to keep a roof over your head. What's happened to the priorities? They've probably turned into a guilt trip and are taking you for a ride.

Hopefully, God is still at the top as you continue to "seek first the kingdom of God" (Matt. 6:33). Or did you temporarily place Him at the bottom because He allowed this terrible thing to happen and you're not even sure you want to be on speaking terms with Him at the moment?

Your husband, because he is in agreement with your working, is still in second place. And your children, now under more of their father's influence as a househusband, will still receive a fair amount of your attention. But people outside your home? Let's face it, even though people are important, in some cases the job will have to take priority.

In another case, a mom is forced to prioritize her job up there along with God and her children—that is, if they want food and a place to sleep. What I'm saying is that we can't afford to live by a rigid set of priorities. We must be flexible to put our strength into the various duties God gives us to carry out. Priorities can and often will change from day to day.

I work out of my home and know that I am being obedient to God's will in this ministry. While I try to maintain a balance between God, family, home, and career, there are times when my work is all-consuming.

If I were to consistently put my job before my family and home, I would be out of balance. Likewise, if I let my writing go and focused all my energies into my family and home (which I could easily do), I would again be out of balance.

When Priorities Go Wrong

Shuffling priorities is fine, as long as you maintain your responsibilities at home and with God. In this busy lifestyle, however, it's easy to wrongly shift our priorities. I know—I've done it.

About two years ago, I became involved in a business. It was a worthwhile venture, and at the time I thought it was right for me. However, I let the business steal time from my family, my writing, and my home. After months of frustration and restlessness, it finally dawned on me that I was off center. I'd put the business first and in doing so had thrown my whole life out of alignment. I had to reprioritize.

Priority living can help us keep on target, but we shouldn't get too legalistic about it. The point I'm trying to stress here is flexibility.

I'm reminded of the controversy between Mary and Martha in Luke 10:38–42. Martha was busy concerning herself over all the things that had to be done and complained about Mary's decision to sit at Jesus' feet. "Martha, dear friend," Jesus said, "you are so upset over all these details! There is really only one thing worth being concerned about. Mary has discovered it—and I won't take it away from her."

As we read in Ecclesiastes, "There is a time for every purpose under heaven." There is a time for sweeping and a time for singing lullabies. There is a time for preparing meals and a time for sitting down together. There is a time for staying home and a time to go out to the fields. There is a time to do dishes and a time to sit at the feet of Jesus.

As mothers and women, let's take care we don't get so involved with our priority list that we forget to listen for that still small voice of God.

The next chapter is titled "Help and Hope for Working Moms." I want to clarify right now that I don't mean just moms who work outside the home. This chapter will be helpful to every busy mother who wishes she had a thirty-six-hour day. So, stay-at-home moms, read on—there's good stuff here for you too.

15

Help and Hope for Working Moms

As I mentioned earlier, half of the mothers in this country are employed outside the home.

Is the Working Mom Living in Sin?

There's been a great deal of controversy over the last few decades about the "working mother." On one extreme we see "liberated" women (usually from the recruiting department of the Super Mom Corps) urging moms to find themselves by leaving the home and getting a job where they can work for money. In the workforce, they say, moms can be appreciated, gain social status, and be able to talk about something other than babies and the latest recipe for broiled prunes at parties.

On the other side we have some religious groups telling moms to return to "traditional family values and get back home where they belong." While the women who work away from home are not exactly shunned, ambivalent feelings hang suspended in an aura of disapproval. Women who work outside the home are somehow less desirable than the traditional stay-at-home mom. "Work if you must," traditionalists say, "but it is, of course, better to stay home and concentrate on rearing your family."

One might get the idea that working at a job outside the home is sinful. What a guilt trip to lay on moms who are already loaded down. If you've been carrying around an extra burden of guilt because you've been told you should be home with your kids, I've got news for you. The stay-at-home, "traditional" mother is a product of our environment—not a commandment from God.

Don't get me wrong. I love the idea of moms being able to stay home. It's just that in this day, when so many mothers are working, we shouldn't keep trying to hold fast to that dream and call it a Christian principle.

Maybe you're thinking this doesn't happen anymore. After all, haven't we come out of the Dark Ages? Yet who gets blamed when a kid turns rebellious? And who gets the finger pointed at her for causing the breakdown of the family? If Mom is working, she often ends up the accused. I've even heard some "experts" come on pretty strong against moms who work outside the home.

One radio pastor even went so far as to call moms who work outside the home "non-mothers."

My good friend Jennifer divorced her husband after enduring years of verbal and physical abuse to herself and her kids. With four children and an ex-husband who contributes child support when he feels like it, she had to find a job.

Her children understand that in order for them to survive, Mom must work. They support her and help her by accepting the inevitable. They are a family pulling together because they have to.

Are we non-mothers simply because we must work outside the home? Are we selfish and materialistic because we want our children to have a place to live and food to fill their tummies? Is it somehow less spiritual or out of God's will to pursue a career outside of the home?

If we were to take this too seriously, we would all end up guilt-ridden zombies. I can't for one minute believe that I've been living in sin because I messed up by being a working mom.

Some moms have no choice but to work. If all the women who were divorced or widowed stayed home, most of them would starve to death or end up bankrupting the welfare program. Nice as it would be to have others take care of you, it is hardly realistic.

Do kids need a mom who stays home all the time to rear them?

To answer that, I'd like you to take a quick look at a very special mom.

Ode to a Working Mom

She finds wool and flax and busily spins it. She buys imported foods, brought by ship from distant ports. She gets up before dawn to prepare breakfast for her household, and plans the day's work for her servant girls. She goes out to inspect a field, and buys it; with her own hands she plants a vineyard. She is energetic, a hard worker, and watches for bargains. She works far into the night!

She sews for the poor, and generously gives to the needy. She has no fear of winter for her household, for she has made warm clothes for all of them. She also upholsters with finest tapestry; her own clothing is beautifully made—a purple gown of pure linen. Her husband is well known, for he sits in the council chamber with the other civic leaders. She makes belted linen garments to sell to the merchants.

She is a woman of strength and dignity, and has no fear of old age. When she speaks, her words are wise, and kindness is the rule for everything she says. She watches carefully all that goes on throughout her household, and is never lazy. Her children stand and bless her; so does her husband. He praises her with these words: "There are many fine women in the world, but you are the best of them all!"

Charm can be deceptive and beauty doesn't last, but a woman who fears and reverences God shall be greatly praised. Praise her for the many fine things she does. These good deeds of hers shall bring her honor and recognition from even the leaders of the nations.

Proverbs 31:13–31 TLB

What you have just read is the classic picture of a working mother. Since I don't like using so many "shes," let's give our lady a name. How about Vera (meaning "strong in virtue")?

Vera, as you may have guessed, was not a stay-at-home mom in the traditional sense.

Who saw to the needs of her children? She did, apparently, because they called her blessed (remind you of Mother's Day?). But you'll notice Vera didn't see to all the needs of the household *alone*. She delegated. Who do you think cared for the children while she was out inspecting and buying land, planting a vineyard, and running her garment factory?

You've got it—the proverbial baby-sitter, who was then a slave or a handmaiden.

Vera had all sorts of interests outside the home. Yet she was still able to mother her children.

I learn from this that there are many more important things children need in a mother besides simply being available at all hours of the day or night to meet their every need and demand.

Can Working Mothers Make Good Moms?

Can working fathers make good dads? I'll let you think about that one for a while. And as you ponder the point, here is an interesting thought about children of working moms.

The Working Mother in America was a comprehensive study regarding maternal employment. Authors concluded that children whose mothers worked outside the home did not suffer maternal deprivation. Nor did they suffer in their growth and development. Actually, these children were found to be more independent and self-sufficient than those whose mothers stayed home.[1]

On the other hand, we have evidence from psychologists and sociologists who maintain that in the earlier years children do better with consistency and a secure home environment. It is obviously more difficult for the working mother to provide as much consistency and security as a stay-at-home mom, since she's actually working two jobs—but it is not impossible.

This book isn't meant to sway you one way or another. Mothers who work away from home are not necessarily going to be rearing juvenile delinquents any more than the stay-at-home moms will be rearing saints.

But there are ways for both types to be the kind of mom their kids need. One of the most important factors for mothers employed outside the home is attitude.

All I Ever Wanted Was to Be a Mom

As a young mother, I believed I should be a stay-at-home mom. My husband and our bank account had other ideas. I had to enter the world of working mothers even though everything in me screamed against it. I felt jealous, bitter, resentful, and angry with my husband, God, and life as a whole, because I was forced to leave partial care of my children in someone else's hands. Finances trapped me into the role of a working mom and I hated it.

It hurt to think that I wasn't indispensable and that I could be even partially replaced, especially in the role of mother. I liked to think that motherhood was the one area where I was truly needed.

It took a while for me to realize the futility of my negative thinking. Unfortunately, friends piled more pities on my party with comments like these:

"The kids really need a mother at home. If you went on a strict budget I'll bet . . ."

"How can you stand not being there to watch them grow up?"

"You wouldn't have to work if you really didn't want to."

Talk about guilt. I thought I was losing out on the best years of my children's lives. I felt miserable and sorry for myself. Even when I was with the kids on weekends and in the evenings, I was so miserable I couldn't enjoy them.

While I still hold to the idea that a mother is a special person in a child's life, I found there were other people who could, under my supervision, attend to our children's needs, leaving me free to do my work without guilt. Once working mothers can gain freedom from the negative feelings of guilt, resentment, and anger, they can relax and have fun with their kids. The transition makes that valuable time we can spend with our children more enjoyable for everyone.

Helps for Moms Who Work Away from Home

If you're working outside the home and would rather be home mothering your kids, consider these possibilities:

1. Ask yourself the question "Do I really have to work?" Discuss the possibility with your husband. You might go so far as to work out a budget to determine just how beneficial your paycheck is to the family. Often women have found that the added expenses of child care, clothing, and extra food costs practically wipe out the profits. They've found that by tightening up on their budgets they can make it on their husband's paycheck. If that's your case, change jobs and go for a full-time career as a homemaker.

2. Another option is to cut back to part-time work. (I'll be sharing more on the freedom of part-time work in the next chapter.)

3. No way out? Maybe you're widowed and your pension isn't enough to keep your bird in seed. Or maybe your husband has said good-bye in court and you haven't seen him since. For many women, depending on child support or alimony is as foolish as expecting to win a million-dollar lottery. Most of them have to work or they don't eat—unless, of course, you find someone who'd like to take care of you.

If you don't come equipped with a benefactor, I suggest you:

- Go ahead and work, but don't fight it. Remember, there are many other women who are on the same crazy merry-go-round. Encourage and support one another.
- Try to maintain a positive attitude. Memorize such Bible verses as Philippians 4:8 TLB: "Fix your thoughts on what is true and good and right. Think about things that are pure and lovely, and dwell on the fine, good things in others. Think about all you can praise God for and be glad about."
- Think of all the positive aspects of being a working mom: (1) the money, (2) you get to eat, (3) your children can become more self-reliant, (4) you'll appreciate your time with them more, (5) your work is helping others, and (6) think of ways God can use your out-of-home time for good. It might help to make a list of all the benefits derived from your being a working mother.
- Ask yourself the question "Do I really like my job or would I be better suited to something else?" Try finding a job that you really enjoy or perhaps one that would allow you to work from your home. I did—I became a writer.

Working in a career that can be managed at home is becoming increasingly popular for mothers. It cuts car, clothing, and child-care expenses.

4. Share the load. If you are a single mom, perhaps you can find another single mother caught in the same sinking ship. You may want to consider the option of sharing a home. That way you can cut expenses and possibly both work part-time. You may even be able to work different shifts and do away with the expense and hassle of child care. Another benefit is that you have more hands to help with housework.

Whether you work in your home or out, job satisfaction is as important to your kids as it is to you. A woman who is unhappy in her job brings her discontentment home and, like a communicable disease, it spreads throughout the house. Wouldn't you rather spread a few germs of joy? Job satisfaction can give you a new respect for yourself, a bounce to your walk, and a smile. Be happy in your situation and your kids will usually catch the bug.

Who Will Care for the Kids?

The big question for moms who work away from home is child care. The problem may be an enormous one. When I first went to work, my baby was only three months old. My husband was attending school, and I had to work. I loved my job, but leaving my baby every morning was the most heart-wrenching thing I've ever had to do. The baby-sitter had several other children. She'd come highly recommended. Yet I knew she didn't change my baby as often as I did. I knew he wasn't getting the attention that I'd have given him. Why? She didn't love my child as much as I did.

Later, when we moved back home, Nana, the children's grandmother, cared for the children. I knew they were getting the kind of care a mother could give because she loved them.

The secret to satisfactory child care is to find someone who loves your child as much as you do—ideally a relative, or perhaps a nanny. Nannies live in the home, do light housework, and often become part of the family.

Besides having our children cared for by Nana, the second-best situation for child care was an elderly neighbor woman, Mrs. Aldinger. Mrs. Aldinger would come to our house before the children came home from school, and she'd stay until my husband or I arrived. She would do light work such as folding clothes and seemed more like a grandmother than a baby-sitter.

Often we had the children go to a neighbor's house after school. She was paid, of course, but she had children as well, and for our kids it was more an afternoon of playing with friends than going to a baby-sitter's house.

Many moms choose to spend one to three years at home with their infants before going back into the workforce. Whenever possible, I'd encourage you to stay home for at least a year. This time is valuable for the special bonding that takes place between the child and the parents.

Many child-development experts attest to the importance of bonding or attachment during the first few years of a child's life. Mother, or a mother figure, is extremely important to a child. There is a general consensus that the child will do best when he or she is cared for by someone who really loves the child.

Now who besides a mother (and maybe a grandma) is going to love a child to distraction? Who besides Mom is going to think your baby is the most beautiful, smartest, most important baby in the world?

Some mothers who do go back to work soon after baby is born have chosen to take their babies with them. One pediatrician I know brought her baby with her to the office and now works on a part-time basis.

Remember the papoose board? Indian mothers had this nifty backpack into which they bundled baby. The child went nearly everywhere the mother did.

We now have baby packs in every shape and color. Our more modern innovations allow mother to carry baby in front or back. Even the busiest moms can keep baby close. So, what if your boss won't allow a baby on the premises? Maybe we mothers need to make employers more aware of the benefits of such a program: (1) Moms will be happier and will probably use less sick leave; (2) babies will probably be more content and secure knowing Mom's right there; and (3) when baby gets too big for the backpack, how about a child-care service right on the premises, so Mom can check on baby during breaks?

Unfortunately, many adults are intolerant when it comes to children. Maybe it's time we let our hair down and accept children into those forbidden places and meetings for grown-ups only. "As long as kids are fairly well behaved, why not take them with you?" my friend Sharon says. "Sometimes I get annoyed glances from people, but I try not to let it bother me. After all, kids are special—they belong. I think we need to reeducate the population to be more tolerant."

Okay, so maybe bringing baby to the job won't work for you. Then I suggest you hire the best person you can find to care for your child. Choose someone with similar values who agrees with and can carry out your techniques for child rearing. Finally, choose someone who loves your child almost as much as you do.

Time for Yourself

Working moms may be under a lot of stress. Time is short and energy may often seem like something you pay the electric company for. It's easy to get so busy you forget to take time to take care of yourself. There are two things I'd encourage you to do for your sake as well as for the sake of your children. First, stay healthy; second, take time to relax with mini-vacations or meditation.

Stay Healthy

A healthy mother is a better mother. Take good care of yourself by eating right and exercising regularly.

Because we are often rushed and because so many of us are on a perpetual diet to keep from gaining weight, we don't always get an adequate supply of vitamins and minerals. I know I'm beginning to sound like an ad for Geritol, but it's true.

If we let ourselves get run down, we become cranky, irritable, depressed, and downright tired. Proper dieting and exercise can eliminate those symptoms and turn you into a happier, well-adjusted mom again.

Take care of yourself. And take care of your children, too. They can suffer from the effects of a poor diet. Overuse of sugar, for example, has been found to cause extreme hyperactivity in some children.

Let's take good care of our bodies and teach our children to as well. When the body we've got wears out, we don't get a replacement.

Meditation Instead of Medication

Stresses can and often do build up to a great big pain in the neck or head. You can often ward off stress simply by taking a few minutes to relax. My advice is not to take two aspirin and call the doctor in the morning. Rather, I'd encourage you to *meditate,* not *medicate.*

For some of you meditation might mean going off to a high mountain to meet with a guru. Not so. By meditation, I simply mean taking time out. Although I firmly believe everyone needs occasional long time-outs such as retreats, a weekend at the beach, a second honeymoon in Bermuda (without the kids), I'd like to take this space to talk about daily breaks or mini-meditations.

Why would a mother need a time for meditation? Let's take a peek at a typical mother around dinnertime:

Donna has just put in six hours cleaning cupboards, washing floors, dusting, and vacuuming—for someone else. (Donna uses her homemaking skills to bring in a little extra income by cleaning for several clients.)

It's time for dinner. The kids—Kevin, who's four, and Brad, who's six, and even Shawn, her one-year-old—are playing quietly in the family room. Could it be that just once she'll be able to prepare dinner without the usual interruptions?

Donna pauses to peer into the family room. The older children are playing with their trucks, and Shawn is busy stuffing his mouth with a giant block. Donna smiles to herself. It would be a miracle, but miracles have been known to happen. She attacks her task with renewed enthusiasm. Maybe she'll even make a hollandaise sauce for the asparagus tonight.

Just as she plops the last few pieces of chicken in the bag for a flour coating, a bloodcurdling scream echoes through the house.

"Boys," she calls out patiently, "give Shawn his teddy bear." She turns to shake the chicken in the bag.

Suddenly Donna is trapped in Kevin's vicelike grip. Her legs have become an unwilling shield as her boys prepare to wage the Civil War all over again. She struggles to walk, but Kevin only holds on tighter, swinging around one leg, like a monkey on a tree limb, as Brad closes in.

"Okay, that's enough," Donna warns. "How many times have I told you not to play in the kitchen while I'm cooking dinner? It's dangerous."

"But, Mom," Kevin whines, "he's trying to hit me."

"No, I'm not. We're just playing."

"Go in the living room and play." Donna finally sets the bag of chicken on the counter and extricates herself from Kevin's hold.

Hands on her hips, she watches the boys run into the other room. Satisfied that they'll stay put at least until she gets the chicken in the oven, Donna turns back to her task.

Just as she picks up the now soggy bag of chicken, a wet hand grasps one of her bare feet. "Ma-a-! I eat."

Donna sets aside her growing anxiety and frustration and coos, "In a few minutes, sweetheart." Then she watches in silent horror as the bag ruptures, spilling flour and chicken all over her blond baby and the kitchen floor.

The rest is a nightmare of baby screams, mother sobs, little-boy giggles, a ringing phone, and a hungry dog who's raced in to salvage the meat.

While not every day is this hectic, and times set aside for meditation won't stop all the frenzy, they can help.

Maybe you're complaining, "Where do I find the time for meditating? I barely have time to brush my teeth." If you fall into the "no time" category, here are a few ideas for taking mini-meditation breaks that you might be able to squeeze in.

1. If you work outside the home, don't try to fix a meal as soon as you get home. Habits are hard to break, but it's possible. You might want to fix a fruit snack for the kids. Then take a rest, put your feet up, and meditate on something. You might want to take a few minutes to read, or just close your eyes and your mind. Or, you may want to use this time to meditate on the kids. It's a perfect time for pure listening.

Put on some soothing background music, relax, and enjoy what they're saying. Don't worry about talking much. Kids are great for filling in gaps in conversation. Then when it's time to start dinner, the kids may be content to stay clear of the kitchen because they got your attention first.

2. If you have someone to watch the kids or if they're old enough to be left on their own for half an hour, take a mini-meditation break in a bubble bath.

I am a firm believer in the "bubble your troubles away" philosophy. It really works. Let the warm water ease away the tension. Feel it warm you all over as you snuggle up to your neck in luxury. Read a good book that takes your mind away from those worrisome tasks.

Sometimes I use my bath time to sort out what I have left to do. Then I list them in order. Other times I'll concentrate on a particular calming Bible verse or sing a song.

3. I learned long ago to use the bathroom for meditation. It's the only place I can legitimately go for privacy. I've been known to offer up a mini-prayer: "We've got about five minutes. Calm me down, Lord. Give me patience . . . and make it snappy."

4. You could take an early-morning break. I used to think I should get up earlier than everyone else so I could have an uninterrupted hour of quiet time. Ideally, during this time, I would pray and read the Bible and organize my day. This is a fine practice for early people.

Unfortunately, I am late people. Life before seven in the morning is nonexistent for me—even if I'm up. The only thing I accomplished with the early-bird routine was to feel guilty because I'd fall asleep reading my Bible. To top it off, I never got anything done on those days because I couldn't stay awake long enough to write a "things to do" list.

I found that my mini-meditation times worked very well, and if I wanted longer periods of quiet time I took time after everyone was in bed. Hmmm. Maybe that's why I could never get up in the morning.

At any rate, kids need a rested, relaxed mom. Take a few minutes out of your hectic day to meditate.

Being a working mother is not so much a fact as it is a process. As a process it is constantly changing and redefining itself. It requires enormous energy, ingenuity, adaptability, and perseverance. Being a working mother is not simply a matter of getting a job and then existing. Or of having children at the optimal time in one's life, given a commitment to a career. It's not, of course, a matter of getting married and just living happily ever after, either. It requires sustained effort and continual reassessment of priorities, needs, and goals. It's a way of life that demands the clarification of shared values and objectives, as well as individual needs and feelings. More than that, it is a continuous commitment to the well-being of loved ones—all the loved ones in the family—including oneself![2]

Now, as promised, we'll get into some more helps for moms who stay home. Often their jobs are no less hectic and difficult than the jobs of moms who work out of the home.

And, just as you moms who stay home may have benefited from some of the ideas in this chapter, I'd like moms who work away from home to read some of the suggestions that follow in the next chapter.

16

For Moms Who Stay Home

Mothering isn't easy for stay-at-home moms either. No one ever said it would be. And if you had any illusions to the contrary, now that a child has entered your life, you know otherwise.

In the last chapter I tried to reduce guilt and give encouragement and help to moms who work away from home or in jobs that keep them from being full-time mothers and homemakers.

Because I'm extolling the virtues of a woman who works outside the home, don't think I'm putting down the woman who chooses the full-time job of mothering. I certainly am not.

Homemaking and child care are a full-time job. Also, many women find it is what they do best. Full-time homemaking certainly should be considered a career.

This isn't a chapter for perfectly happy stay-at-home moms; rather it is for moms who want to stay home but feel lacking. They understand the need to be available to their kids, yet harbor feelings of disillusionment, unfulfillment, and loneliness. They are full-time mothers and enjoy it, but something is missing.

Maybe, like my friend Joan, you decided to stay home to rear your kids, but things haven't worked out quite as you planned. Joan complains of feeling trapped. "I don't understand it. I really like being home. I guess I came into the situation of being a stay-at-home mom with rose-colored glasses. I laughed at women who said I'd get bored. At first, my kids really needed me and I loved it. Now that my kids are in school, I find myself wanting something besides romance novels, soaps, and TV talk shows to fill my days. It's not that I don't have housework I could be doing—I just don't want to do it."

Remember when we talked about priorities and the necessity of reevaluating from time to time? That is exactly where Joan is. When her children were small, staying at home and being a full-time wife and mother were fine, but now she needs more.

In addition, Joan has begun to see women who have careers outside the home as being somehow more glamorous than she is. And I suppose meeting clients over lunch, flying a customer into the remote regions of Brazil, signing a contract for a series of six romantic novels, jetting off to Europe to buy the latest fashions for your very own boutique, could be considered more glamorous than mopping floors and wiping runny noses. Unfortunately most jobs, whether homemaking, typing letters, answering phones, or directing movies, get to be tiring after a while.

If you are experiencing some of Joan's frustrations or have begun to see caring for children and home as drudgery, it may be time for a change. Too much of one thing can make a mom feel lonely, left out, worthless, and caged. Just as women who work may have to change their attitudes about their jobs, moms who stay home may, as well.

Having outside interests can greatly improve one's attitude.

Not Only a Mother

There are some women who have chosen to be the World's Greatest Mother. Their concentration on that goal has kept them too busy to pursue other interests.

Hopefully, children will ultimately leave the nest. Then what? Where does a mother go who's had nothing but her kids? There are many women who come to the end of their reproductive cycle depressed, dejected, and devastated.

Children need a mother who has interests outside of them. Kids take pride in watching a mother blossom and grow. As you find new interests, you are teaching your children by example that we never stop learning.

As an artist, I could escape from the pressures of life and throw my frustrations into a creative outlet. When my children were very small, I neglected that very important part of me. For a time, I gave up my art because I thought I should, since I had so little time. I became restless and unhappy and finally realized what had gone wrong. I am not only a mother but an artist as well. It is within my nature to create. God didn't intend that I give up this important part of me for the sake of my kids. He intended that I use my talents for my benefit as well as theirs.

I began taking art classes. My stress levels dropped considerably and my attitude levels rose. And the bonus is that my kids have learned from my art.

As a nurse, I shared with them about illness, caring for people, and caring for themselves. They learned about compassion.

As a writer, I express myself. I am open and honest. They share in my writing by letting me use their stories. They write journals, poetry, and sometimes prose to express their feelings. They learned from my craft. They are proud to have a "famous" mom.

My children didn't suffer from my outside interests—I set my projects aside when they needed me. They grew more independent and self-assured. Now, with my nest empty, I don't pine away longing for the sound of children. I'm busy because I enjoy my own interests.

We have an appeal from God to build our home and maintain order there (see Titus 2:5). We also have an appeal from God in other parts of Scripture to use our unique gifts and talents, to feed the hungry and clothe the naked, to uplift, encourage, and support others. And finally, we have the ultimate task of making disciples of all nations.

So, when we explore the Scriptures as a whole, women are not simply lumped together in one batch of clay. God did not mass-produce us as vessels with one purpose and engrave us with the name "Homemaker." He made each of us with separate and unique abilities. We are apostles, prophets, teachers, healers, miracle workers, administrators . . . (see 1 Cor. 12:28).

We don't stay home because the Bible says we should, and we don't work outside the home because the Bible says we should. The Bible shows women in various situations. Consequently, the answer as to whether or not you should be working outside the home is strictly between you and your family and God.

A child doesn't necessarily need a mom who stays home or one with a job away from home. I've seen neglected and abused children coming out of both situations. I've seen working moms suffer the tragedy of teenage rebellion as their kids choose drugs and alcohol and street gangs over common sense. But I've seen stay-at-home moms suffer the same pain. What kids really need is a mother who loves them enough to be herself.

Do You Need a Change?

Are you needing or wanting to make some changes in your status as a stay-at-home mom? Here are a few considerations you might want to make.

1. Do you really want to stay home? One young mother, Andrea, had a difficult time coming to terms with this question. Andrea, a schoolteacher, decided she would be a stay-at-home mother. For years, she crusaded for mothers who, like herself, felt that being home with the children was essential to their well-being.

> When I started getting restless and thinking how nice it would be to teach again, I really felt guilty. It took a long time for me to realize I was just kidding myself. I wasn't staying home because the kids needed me there. I refused to think about going back to teaching because I didn't want to face the people. After being too adamant about staying home, I'd look like a fool to my friends. After a year of misery and soul-searching, I found the root of my problem: pride.
>
> Once I admitted my need for a change, I felt freedom to go on with my teaching. And, wonder of wonders, I got a call from an old friend who asked me if I'd be interested in tutoring. I love it. I can stay home and work at the same time.

2. Remember that your decision to stay home with your children is not set in concrete. Times change and so do you. Be open for what God might want in your life.

3. Consider what you'll be giving up if you decide to go to work. What effect will your absence have on your family?

4. Consider other options, such as volunteer work for an hour or two a day. Volunteer work gets you out of the house. Helping others is definitely uplifting.

5. Make a list of your feelings about staying home. Write the benefits on one side and the disadvantages on the other. Often, by writing out the pros and cons, you can come to a decision.

6. You may want to talk with a friend about your dilemma.

7. What is the desire of your heart?

8. Be flexible. At this point I'd like to tell you about a woman who loves being a mom, yet mothering isn't her only love.

My friend Sharon, then mother of three small children, had been a home-based, part-time political activist for years.

She got tired of fighting causes and backed off from any and all political involvement. She dedicated her energies to mothering, home schooling her kids, gardening, and homemaking. But God had something different in mind.

"I thought you loved staying at home. What made you decide to run for office?" I asked over lunch one afternoon.

Sharon shrugged. "I began feeling restless. I knew God was urging me to do something—I just couldn't figure out what. After all, I thought I was supposed to be right here at home, taking care of my family. At first I resisted the feelings, but they just got stronger. Then finally, I gave in and said, 'Okay, Lord, what do You want me to do?'"

"And He told you to go to work?"

"When the message came through I was sure I'd misunderstood. But eventually I realized God was urging me to run for the state senate seat."

"How did you know it was God?" I asked.

"I know this may sound strange, but since I didn't particularly want to go I just prayed, 'Lord, if this is really You, You'll have to tell Randy.'

"Then I put the thoughts aside because I knew Randy [her husband] would never agree. I couldn't believe it when he came to me a few days later and said, 'You're running for state senate, aren't you?' I knew. God wanted me to go. I felt at peace again for the first time in months."

"Campaigning takes a lot of time. How did your family do?"

"Not so great at first. Running for senator is no small feat. But three weeks after I registered, a man from church told me he'd been fighting with God for days because he didn't want to get involved. He finally agreed to be my campaign manager. This guy had no previous experience or interest in politics. Anyway, he organized my campaign and got two groups of women to volunteer to watch my kids and clean house. I was given a wardrobe and the use of a car. We fought a good campaign and gave the incumbent a lot of sleepless nights. We nearly made it."

"But you lost. Since God was behind the whole thing, how could that be?"

"I don't think I was meant to be a senator right then. What running did was qualify me as a politician. People don't look at me as 'just a housewife' anymore. The campaign served as a catalyst for moving a lot of Christians into action to help change laws. Shortly after the election I was elected State Committee Woman for our county and elected to the Executive Board of the State Republican Party. Also, I was asked to serve on the U.S. Commission on Civil Rights—Washington State Advisory Board. Through involvement in my campaign, a political-action committee was set up.

"I work to educate and groom people who care and want to see laws changed and our freedoms maintained."

"Wow," I said, "you're doing more now than you could have as a state senator."

"I know . . . isn't God great?"

Sharon shifted priorities and listened to God.

Through her willingness to change priorities, she set an example for Christians in our community, who are realizing the importance of being attuned to and becoming involved with political affairs.

I don't want you to think I'm stressing that all stay-at-home moms should hit the campaign trail or go off to work. I only challenge you to look carefully at the present as well as the future and be open to new vistas.

I like to look at motherhood in terms of the seasons. Each season brings about changes, not only in the kids, but in us moms as well. If you're feeling stagnant in your role as a mother, maybe it's because the season has changed, but you haven't.

Changing with the Seasons

Spring begins with the birth of the first child and lasts until the youngest starts school.

Summer runs through the children's grade-school years, and fades into Fall when your children hit their teens.

Fall lasts until all the kids are grown and gone.

Winter comes when the nest is empty. It begins when the youngest child leaves home.

In Spring, moms will do well to direct most of their energies toward their growing children. Many of the mothers who experience feelings of isolation and disillusionment about motherhood are those who give up everything for the sake of rearing their children. Although some sacrifice is essential, especially during baby's first year, being a mother doesn't supersede who you are. Even during phase one, you can plan some activities. I would simply encourage you to grow as your children grow. Being a mom offers a perfect environment for personal growth.

In Summer, while children are in school, you may want to indulge in an extracurricular activity, perhaps take a class or two, work part-time, do volunteer work. This will give you a new frontier, offer a challenge, and still give you the freedom to be home when the kids are. Summer isn't a time when the kids will need you less—on the contrary, in many ways they'll need you more. But there are more blocks of free time when the kids are in school or playing.

In Fall, it's important that you be there as a mom. You might think that if you had more time when the kids were in grade school, you can count on even more free time during their teen years. Not so. Perhaps more than any of the seasons, it's a time for understanding and unconditional love. Even though your teenagers will often seem too busy to even notice whether or not you're gone, believe me, they'll notice. This isn't the time to take on too much extra work. I was working part-time while my children were in their teens. At times even that seemed too much.

Yet there is still time, during school and when they're gone, to pursue your other interests.

Then there's Winter. The kids are gone and you can move into whatever gear you want: full-time work, part-time, hobbies, volunteer work. But whatever you do, if you've prepared the way, you'll find the empty nest won't hurt so much or feel quite so empty. This is a season for you to come into full bloom. Winter isn't the end—it's just the beginning.

Motherhood never ends; it just turns with the seasons.

Support for Sagging Souls

No matter what the season, or what your situation, I would encourage all moms to be part of a support group. Whether it's a once-a-week Bible study or a once-a-month coffee klatch, I urge you to get together with other mothers.

There is a nationwide support group called MOPS, Inc. (Mothers of Preschoolers). MOPS is a church-sponsored organization, but it is nondenominational and open to everyone. Twice a month or so, moms get together to hear speakers, learn more about mothering, encourage one another, and give support. As one mom said, "It's so good just to know my kid isn't the only one who bites his little sister."

While moms are learning and growing, so are the children. Baby-sitting services (where children play and do crafts) are provided.

A support group lets you know you are not alone. It provides an outlet for a mother's frustrations and a solution to the problem of isolation. For more information on a group in your area or how to get one started, write to:

MOPS
1311 South Clarkson Street
Denver, CO 80210
(303) 733-5353

In the next chapter we'll explore another view of the seasons as we consider the growth and development of a mom.

17

The Growth and Development of a Mom

If I could tell new mothers something for which they'd be eternally grateful, it would be to approach motherhood as a child. Mothers who enter motherhood as if they know all there is to know will miss some of life's most important lessons. Come into motherhood with the awe, the excitement, and the willingness to learn a whole new way of life. Come with the anticipation of a child on his or her first day of school. Isaiah 11:6 KJV says, "a little child shall lead them." Let your children lead and teach you, 'cause, Mama—we've got a lot to learn.

Motherhood is not only a time to watch our children grow but to experience growth ourselves. Grow with me as we walk through the seasons of a mother's life.

Lessons in Springtime

Motherhood is a seed that begins inside us—a new life, waiting to be born. Spring brings freshness to life. Everything is new and clean and full of happiness and hope. The seed takes hold and begins to grow.

In time the child bursts out to meet the world. Spring is a chance to start over—to bend and mold a tiny babe into the grown-up image of God.

It is a joyful time, a new beginning—full of hope and future dreams.

I love Springtime. Or maybe I just love babies. Even now, every time I hold a new baby, the old yearning starts all over again.

But babies don't stay babies. Around two years of age a strange phenomenon takes place. That darling little dependent squirt learns three words that threaten to change your life: *Me do it.*

He's the little guy who fills your sink to overflowing, then innocently looks up at you and says, "Me help." And she's the one who goes into the bathroom and takes her training pants off in front of the potty, just like Mama said. Then she decides to take a walk and piddles all over the house. They are terrible, delightful, exciting, wonder-filled babes who need to explore and test their world.

But somewhere after two and before thirteen, innocence fades and babies stretch into Summer. Walk slowly through Springtime. Let baby teach you how to coo and goo and laugh. Listen closely as he learns to turn sounds into words, and watch as he makes the world his.

> Cleaning and scrubbing can wait 'til tomorrow . . .
> For babies grow up we've learned to our sorrow . . .
> So quiet down, cobwebs . . .
> Dust, go to sleep . . .
> I'm rocking my baby and babies don't keep.
>
> Anonymous

Slow Down Summer

Summer is a time for planting, watering, and nourishing—a time for growing wild like weeds.

Summer is a time for families and fun, games, water fights, and exploring the wonders of the world.

In Summer, I planted seeds of love, joy, peace, patience, kindness, goodness, faithfulness, gentleness, and self-control. I watered the seeds of my labor with the source of my strength—faith in God. I knew I would reap what I sowed, and I prayed for a bountiful harvest.

But Summer days weren't always sunny. Rainstorms, thunder, wind, and the tragedies of nature came to steal my joy. Some of the seeds I planted weren't good. I didn't mean to, but sometimes I sowed seeds of anger, discontent, frustration, selfishness.

In the Summer of my motherhood, I had moments of selfishness and anger. Sometimes I was too busy. I thought the children had all the time in the world. But they grow so fast in Summer.

Slow down your Summer. Don't let the days slip by too fast. Sometimes I wish we could go back to when Summer meant sipping sodas in the shade of the old oak tree instead of racing around to see how many things we can get done while the sun's still out.

Summer is the greatest time for learning mothers. Take advantage of all a child has to teach you. Go outside with Casey on a Summer day and let him show you how to spend half the day doing absolutely nothing. Nothing, that is, except:

- Watch an ant move a mountain twice its size.
- Make music with a blade of grass.
- Chase a butterfly across an open field.
- Skip rocks in a bubbly stream.

Naturally, you can't spend all your days that way. But take at least an hour or two one day a week to spend with your child and do absolutely "nothing."

Too soon Summer is over and we slip into Fall.

Reaping Summer's Harvest

A mother's Fall brings the harvest. The time has come to reap what we have sown. Nature has matured. Seedlings drop or fly away to start life on their own.

In Autumn moms learn what it's like to experience the growing pains of adolescence. Take the time to feel and understand the changes and confusion in your teenagers. Let yourself hurt and cry and laugh with them. Some of the best times of my motherhood have been sharing the pain and joy as I watched my children mature into adults, while I grew and developed as a mother.

I was like a maple tree. Back in Spring my branches had burst forth with new life from inside me. I pulled from the well within me and from whatever I could reach around me to nourish them, to help them grow.

Then Autumn winds grew strong, and my branches held mature seedlings. Nature brought the winds and stripped my branches clean. My babies have been whisked away on the winds of life.

Will they survive?

Will they be carried on the wind into dangerous ground?

Will they settle among the thorns and be choked out?

Will they fall on fertile ground?

Autumn was a time for wondering where I had gone right—or wrong. It was a time of anticipation and guilt. I think perhaps the harvest was the hardest time of all.

When they all have flown away . . .

Growing in Winter

Barren branches. Empty nests. Winter is a time to wait and watch for signs of spring. Sometimes in Winter loneliness reaches inside me like an icy hand and holds me in its frozen grip.

The children have grown and gone; they are living lives of their own.

In Winter I have learned I was not all wrong. And guilt is a thing to be forgiven and forgotten. I watch as Winter snows cover my scars. Even mothers take a lot of spills. God in His grace heals all wounds. And I pause to thank Him.

I wait and watch. Someday, maybe another seed is sown. Another baby born—a grandchild of my very own.

A new life, a new beginning, new hope. Another Spring. Another mother sees the fruit of her labor.

What Kids Need Most . . .

We've covered a lot of territory in learning about what kids need most in a mom. I suppose if I were to choose the three most important things moms can give their kids they would be:

Learning . . . to always keep an open mind and heart for what children and life can teach you.

Living . . . a life in day-to-day anticipation of what each new moment might bring. Living to fulfill the needs of those you love—yourself included.

Loving . . . with a wide, unconditional love that knows no boundaries and has no end.

What do *your* kids need most in a mom? You.

Notes

Chapter 2   The Mythical, Mystical, Magical Mom

1. Marjorie P. Katz and Jean S. Arbeiter, *Pegs to Hang Ideas On* (New York: M. Evans and Company, 1973), 30.

2. Erma Bombeck, *Motherhood: The Second Oldest Profession* (New York: Dell Publishing Co., Inc., 1983), 25–27.

Chapter 3   Real Moms Don't Eat Baby Food

1. Rudolph Schaffer, *Mothering* (Cambridge, Mass.: Harvard University Press, 1977).

2. Katz and Arbeiter, *Pegs to Hang Ideas On,* 37.

3. The segment, Make Room for Daddy, was adapted from an article appearing as "Daddy's Turn," by Patricia H. Rushford in *Christian Parenting Today,* Sept./Oct. 1993, 17.

4. The segment, Realize How Important Dads Are, was adapted from an article appearing as "Daddy Time," by Patricia H. Rushford in *New Man,* July/Aug. 1995, 92–93.

5. Katz and Arbeiter, *Pegs to Hang Ideas On,* 37.

Chapter 4   The Trouble with Super Moms

1. Patricia H. Rushford, *Have You Hugged Your Teenager Today?* (Grand Rapids: Revell, 1983), 18–20.

2. Glenn Doman, "Bringing up Baby," *Newsweek,* March 28, 1983, 62–68.

3. Ibid.

4. Raymond Moore, Ed.D., *School Can Wait* (Provo, Utah: Brigham Young University Press, 1979).

Chapter 5   If Time Were Diamonds

1. "Jean Lush Talks to Mothers," *Focus on the Family,* James Dobson Interview #618, © 1982.

Chapter 6   A Room Full of Memories

1. Eugenia Smith-Durland, *Voluntary Simplicity: Study Action Guide* (Forest Park, Ga.: Alternatives, 1978), 49.

Chapter 7   In the Heart of a Stone

1. M. Scott Peck, M.D., *The Road Less Traveled* (New York: Simon & Schuster, Inc., 1978), 121.
2. Ibid., 127–28.

Chapter 8   Weaving in the Threads of Discipline

1. Dr. James Dobson, *Dare to Discipline* (Wheaton, Ill.: Tyndale House, 1970), 21.
2. Gregory Bodenhamer, *Back in Control* (Englewood Cliffs, N.J.: Prentice-Hall, Inc., 1983), 11.
3. Janet Pais, *Suffer the Children* (New York: Paulist Press, 1991), 130.
4. Edith Schaeffer, *What Is a Family?* (Grand Rapids: Revell, 1975), 74.

Chapter 11   The Library

1. Gladys Hunt, *Honey for a Child's Heart* (Grand Rapids: Zondervan, 1969), 14.
2. Ibid., 21.
3. *The Parent Educator and Family Report,* May/June 1985, 5–6.
4. Peck, *The Road Less Traveled,* 15.

Chapter 12   The Throne Room

1. Peck, *The Road Less Traveled,* 81.
2. Ibid., 119.
3. David Augsburger, *Caring Enough to Forgive* (Ventura, Calif.: Regal Books, 1981).

Chapter 13   The Servant's Quarters

1. William Barclay, *The Gospel of John,* vol. 2 of *The Daily Bible Study Series* (Philadelphia: The Westminster Press, 1975), 137.

Chapter 15   Help and Hope for Working Moms

1. Maxine L. Margolis, *Mothers and Such* (Berkeley: University of California Press, 1984), 84.
2. Jeanne Bodin and Bonnie Mitelman, *Mothers Who Work: Strategies for Coping* (New York: Ballantine Books, 1983), 231.

Suggested Reading List

Books for Kids

Danis, Naomi. *Walk with Me.* New York: Scholastic, 1995. A toddler and a caring adult walk together in their neighborhood, experiencing sights and sounds of the outdoors, then return to the comfort of their house.

Haidle, Helen, ed. *What Would Jesus Do?* Charles M. Sheldon's classic *In His Steps* retold for children. Portland, Ore.: Multnomah, 1997.

Other children's titles by Helen Haidle include:

Angels in Action. Nashville: Thomas Nelson, 1996.

Candy Cane Christmas. St. Louis: Concordia, 1997.

The Candymaker's Gift: The Inspirational Legend of the Candy Cane. Tulsa: Honor Books, 1996.

The First Christmas Tree. Grand Rapids: Baker, 1997.

God Made Me. St. Louis: Concordia, 1997.

He Is My Shepherd: The Twenty-Third Psalm for Children. Sisters, Ore.: Multnomah, 1989.

Pocket Full of Parables. Sisters, Ore.: Multnomah, 1995.

Pocket Full of Praises. Sisters, Ore.: Multnomah, 1995.

Pocket Full of Prayer. Sisters, Ore.: Multnomah, 1995.

Pocket Full of Promises. Sisters, Ore.: Multnomah, 1995.

Pocket Full of Proverbs. Sisters, Ore.: Multnomah, 1995.

Pocket Full of Psalms. Sisters, Ore.: Multnomah, 1995.

The Real Twelve Days of Christmas. Sisters, Ore.: Multnomah, 1998.

Sing Me to Sleep & Wake Me with a Song. Sisters, Ore.: Multnomah, 1996.

Sleepy-Time Rhymes. Eugene, Ore.: Harvest House, 1998.

Joosse, Barbara M. *Mama, Do You Love Me?* San Francisco: Chronicle Books, 1991. A delightful story about a mother's unconditional love.

Kasza, Keiko. *A Mother for Choco.* New York: G. P. Putnam's Sons, 1992. Choco, a lonely bird, wishes for a mother. After meeting many animals, none of which look like him, he finds Mrs. Bear. Even though she looks different from Choco, Mrs. Bear does all the warm, comforting things that a mother would do.

Kondracki, Linda. She has written a series of books that encourages interaction between parents and children to help them understand their feelings (published by Revell, Grand Rapids).

All My Feelings Are Okay. 1993.

Going Through Change Together. 1996.

I Always, Always Have Choices. 1992.

Let's Talk, Let's Listen Too. 1993.

Larson, Elsie. *Bombus the Bumblebee.* Green Forest, Ark.: Master Books, 1997.

———. *Bombus Finds a Friend.* Green Forest, Ark.: Master Books, 1998. There will soon be a Bombus activity book with the two story books containing activities for children ages four to eight.

McBratney, Sam. *Guess How Much I Love You.* Cambridge, Mass.: Candlewick Press, 1995. There is a deep tender bond between Little Nutbrown Hare and Big Nutbrown Hare in this touching story that makes wonderful bedtime reading.

Murphy Payne, Lauren. *Just Because I Am: A Child's Book of Affirmation.* Minneapolis: Free Spirit Publishing, 1994.

Books for Parents

Barron-Tieger, Barbara. *Nurture by Nature: Understanding Your Child's Personality Type—and Become a Better Parent.* Boston: Little, Brown & Co., 1997.

Boyd, Charles F., with David Boehi. *Different Children Different Needs: The Art of Adjustable Parenting.* Portland, Ore.: Multnomah, 1994.

Brazelton, T. Berry, M.D. *Touchpoints: Your Child's Emotional and Behavioral Development.* Reading, Mass.: Addison-Wesley Longman, 1994.

Brazo, Carol J. *No Ordinary Home: The Uncommon Art of Christ-Centered Home-Making*. Sisters, Ore.: Questar Publishers, 1995.

Chapman, Gary D. *The Five Love Languages of Children*. Chicago: Moody, 1997.

Cline, Foster W., M.D. *Parenting with Love and Logic: Teaching Children Responsibility*. Colorado Springs: Pinon Press, 1990.

Coles, Robert. *The Moral Intelligence of Children: How to Raise a Moral Child*. New York: Random House, 1998.

———. *The Spiritual Life of Children*. Boston: Houghton Mifflin, 1990.

Davis, Laura, and Janis Keyser. *Becoming the Parent You Want to Be: A Sourcebook of Strategies for the First Five Years*. New York: Broadway Books, 1997.

Dobson, James. *Dare to Discipline*. Wheaton: Tyndale House, 1970.

———. *The New Hide or Seek*. Grand Rapids: Revell, 1999.

———. *The Strong-Willed Child: Parenting Isn't for Cowards*. New York: Budget Book Service, 1997.

Endicott, Irene. *Grandparenting by Grace*. Nashville: Broadman & Holman, 1994.

Evans, Debra, ed. *Christian Parenting Answers: Before Birth to Five Years*. Colorado Springs: Christian Parenting Books (Imprint of David C. Cook, Elgin, Ill.), 1994. Contains works from Dr. William Sears, Dr. Grace Ketterman, V. Gilbert Beers, Mary Manz Simon, Dr. Kay Kuzma, Patricia H. Rushford, and more.

Eyer, Diane. *Mother Guilt: How Our Culture Blames Mothers for What's Wrong with Society*. New York: Random House, 1997.

Eyre, Linda. *I Didn't Plan to Be a Witch and Other Surprises of a Joyful Mother*. New York: Simon & Schuster, 1988, 1996. We've all had days when we feel like the world's wickedest witch, when nothing seems to go right. At the end of such a day, we feel exhausted from the struggle and saddened by the way we interacted with our kids.

Ezzo, Gary, and Robert Bucknam. *On Becoming Baby Wise. Book Two: Parenting Your Pre-Toddler Five to Fifteen Months*. Sisters, Ore.: Multnomah, 1995.

Ford, Judy, MSW. *Wonderful Ways to Love a Child*. Berkeley: Conari Press, 1995. Judy Ford describes her book as "a guide for parents who want to put love into action so they can give their children the very best start in life. It's a prescription to strengthen your family, packed with guidance and reassurance and filled with true stories from parents who are building strong, nurturing, loving families." This is a wonderful book for parents of children of any age.

Fraiberg, Selma H. *The Magic Years: Understanding and Handling the Problems of Early Childhood*. New York: Scribner, 1996.

Giannetti, Charlene C., and Margaret Sagarese. *The Roller-Coaster Years: Raising Your Child through the Maddening Yet Magical Middle School Years.* New York: Broadway Books, 1997.

Gottman, John. *The Heart of Parenting: How to Raise an Emotionally Intelligent Child.* New York: HarperCollins, Simon & Schuster, 1997.

Greenspan, Stanley I., M.D., et al. *The Child with Special Needs: Encouraging Intellectual and Emotional Growth.* Reading, Mass.: Addison-Wesley Longman, 1996, 1998.

Hansel, Tim. *What Kids Need Most in a Dad.* Grand Rapids: Revell, 1984, 1989.

Hendrix, Harville. *Giving the Love That Heals: A Guide for Parents.* New York: Pocket, 1997.

Ketterman, Dr. Grace H. *The Complete Book of Baby and Child Care.* Grand Rapids: Revell, 1982, 1985.

Lansky, Vicki. *101 Ways to Be a Special Mom.* Lincolnwood: NTC/Contemporary Publishing Co., 1988.

Littauer, Florence. *Personality Plus.* Grand Rapids: Revell, 1983, 1992.

Looney, Cornelia, and Douglas S. Looney. *All for the Love of a Child: A Memoir.* Birmingham, Ala.: Crane Hill Publishing, 1997.

Lush, Jean, and Patricia H. Rushford. *Emotional Phases of a Woman's Life.* Grand Rapids: Revell, 1987.

McCormick, Calkins, and Lucy Lydia Bellino. *Raising Lifelong Learners: A Parent's Guide.* Reading, Mass.: Addison-Wesley Longman, 1997.

Miller-McLemore, Bonnie J. *Also a Mother: Work & Family as Theological Dilemma.* Nashville: Abingdon Press, 1994.

Newenhuyse, Elizabeth Cody. *Am I the Only Crazy Mom on This Planet?* Grand Rapids: Zondervan, 1994.

Newman, Susan. A leading social psychologist, she is the author of numerous books on parenting including:

Let's Always . . . Promises to Make Love Last. New York: Berkley/Putnam, 1995.

Little Things Long Remembered: Making Your Children Feel Special Every Day. New York: Random House/Crown, 1993.

Little Things Mean a Lot: Creating Happy Memories with Your Grandchildren. New York: Random House/Crown, 1996.

Little Things Shared: Lasting Connections between Family and Friends. New York: Random House/Crown, 1998.

Parenting an Only Child: The Joys and Challenges of Raising Your One and Only. New York: Doubleday, 1990; reissued, 1994.

Ortlund, Anne. *Children Are Wet Cement.* Grand Rapids: Revell, 1981.

Peters, Joan K. *When Mothers Work: Loving Our Children without Sacrificing Our Selves.* New York: Addison-Wesley, 1997.

Porter, Dahlia, and Gabriel Cervantes. *365 Reflections on Mothers.* Holbrook, Mass.: Adams Media Corp., 1998.

Ramming, Cindy. *All Mothers Work: A Guilt-Free Guide for the Stay-at-Home Mom.* New York: Avon, 1996.

Rice, Wayne. *Enjoy Your Middle Schooler: A Guide to Understanding the Physical, Social, Emotional, and Spiritual Changes of Your 11–14-Year-Old.* Grand Rapids: Zondervan, 1994.

Rushford, Patricia H. *Have You Hugged Your Teenager Today?* Grand Rapids: Revell, 1983, rev. ed., 1996.

———. *The Jack and Jill Syndrome: Healing for Broken Children.* Grand Rapids: Revell, 1996.

St. James, Elaine. *Simplify Your Life with Kids: 100 Ways to Make Family Life Easier and More Fun.* Kansas City: Andrews & McMeel, 1997.

Shelov, Steven P., and Robert E. Hannemann. *Caring for Your Baby and Young Child: Birth to Age 5* (The American Academy of Pediatrics). New York: Bantam, 1998.

Simon, Mary Manz. *How to Parent Your 'Tweenager'/Understanding the In-Between Years of Your 8- to 12-Year-Old.* Nashville: Thomas Nelson, 1995.

Strickland, Guy. *Bad Teachers: The Essential Guide for Concerned Parents.* New York: Pocket Books, 1998.

Tobias, Cynthia. *Every Child Can Succeed: Making the Most of Your Child's Learning Style.* Colorado Springs: Focus on the Family Publishing, 1996.

———. *The Way They Learn.* Colorado Springs: Focus on the Family Publishing, 1995; Wade Cook Seminars, 1996.

Tobias, Cynthia, and Carol Funk. *Bringing Out the Best in Your Child: 80 Ways to Focus on Every Kid's Strengths.* Ann Arbor, Mich.: Servant Publications, 1997.

Vannoy, Steven W. *The 10 Greatest Gifts I Give My Children: Parenting from the Heart.* 1994.

Willis, Kay, and Maryann B. Brinley. *Are We Having Fun Yet?: The 16 Secrets of Happy Parenting.* New York: Warner Books, 1998.

Wright, Judy. *Kids, Chores & More: How to Get Your Kids to Help at Home.* Missoula, Mont.: Laurel E. Press, 1994.

Internationally known author and speaker Patricia H. Rushford has book sales totaling over three-quarters of a million copies. She has written numerous articles and authored more than thirty books, including *Have You Hugged Your Teenager Today?* and *The Jack and Jill Syndrome: Healing for Broken Children.* She also writes mystery series for adults and kids; the second book in the Jennie McGrady series for children was nominated for an Edgar by the Mystery Writers of America and another won the Phantom Friends Award.

Patricia is a registered nurse and holds a master's degree in counseling. In addition, she conducts writers' workshops for adults and children and is codirector of *Writer's Weekend at the Beach.* Pat has appeared on numerous radio and television talk shows across the U.S. and Canada. She lives in the Portland, Oregon, area with her husband of thirty-five years; she has two adult children and nine grandchildren.